Spellbound

Floral Beaded

Jewellery

A Spellbound Bead Co Book
Copyright © Spellbound Bead Co Publishing 2016

First Published in the UK 2016
This impression made in the UK 2017

Printed in the UK by WM Print
for Spellbound Bead Co

ISBN - 978-0-9565030-7-7

10 9 8 7 6 5 4 3 2

Editor: Jean Hall
Pattern Testing and Sample Production: Edna Kedge and Victoria Pritchard
Photography: Spellbound Bead Co

Visit our website at www.spellboundbead.co.uk

Spellbound Bead Co
47 Tamworth Street
Lichfield
Staffordshire
WS13 6JW
England

Call 01543 417650 for direct sales
or your local wholesale distributor

Also available by this author:

Spellbound Festive Beading
ISBN 978-0-9565030-2-2

Spellbound Festive Beading Two
ISBN 978-0-9565030-5-3

Spellbound Beaded Tassels
ISBN 978-0-9565030-4-6

Acknowledgements

A special thank you to everyone who has contributed to this book - those who have tested, proofed and taken endless photos, have been patient with a befuddled author and, of course, counted an enormous amount of beads.
Also a big thank you to all of our wonderful customers who bead with such enthusiasm, creativity and joy.
For Mum and Dad.

Contents

The Chapters

To watch a bee collecting plump pollen grains from a plume of powdery stamens, or see the crumpled petals of a new bud unfurl into velvety perfection, is a privilege we take for granted.

How can we fail to be amazed that the apparently delicate blossoms of cherry trees can withstand sudden rain showers that send us running for cover, or when tightly permed curls of woodland ferns slowly unwind under the fingers of springtime sunlight.

Architects take inspiration from gossamer-thin petals that withstand the weight of a bumblebee; leaves that fan out to many hundred times the width of their stem and the minuscule iridescent tiling of scales on a butterfly wing.

This collection is a beader's tribute to the little miracles found in every garden, flower pot and wayside verge.

Some of the projects in this book are favourite designs from past years but the majority are newly-created.

Each chapter starts with a main project which introduces the theme and takes you step-by-step through the construction process.
Some of the chapters then lead on to more elaborate Inspirations projects where a motif or technique from the main project is expanded or adapted. Sometimes there is a simple, additional idea to start you along your own garden path of creativity.

The more complicated Inspirations projects are set out with step-by-step instructions, but it would be good practice to work through the first project in the chapter first. You will find that the Inspirations instructions refer to the first project in the chapter for basic techniques and to illustrate the order of work. The Inspirations all use the same basic tools as the headline project.

Look out for the Extra Info boxes. They contain hints and tips on the techniques and materials you will be using in the projects.

There are flowers with sparkling faceted glass petals, arching stems of nodding bluebells, plump sunflowers and fat-bottomed bees.

Exquisite blossoms on elegant branches and tiny daffodils bring the colours of springtime to the beadwork.

Jewel-coloured butterflies flutter amongst chapters of sumptuous Wisteria blooms and teal green fern leaves.

There's even a little beehive home to hold a tiny treasure or your bee earrings.

It has been wonderful to have a real excuse for spending so much time in the garden. 'Research' I have found, is a marvellous word. I hope you have even more enjoyment on your own 'research' missions choosing beads to make your favourites from the collection.

Now all we need is some sunshine.....

Happy beading,

Julie

All of the main projects are graded for difficulty. Count the number of rosebuds alongside the chapter title and compare them to the grading list below. If you want a really easy project to get started, try the simple leaf and daisy motifs on pages 14 and 15. There are basic instructions for adding a bead and loop clasp on page 9 so you can start designing floral jewellery straight-away.

Choose a Project to Suit Your Beading Experience

 Two Rosebuds - simple techniques repeated several times to build up the design.

 Three Rosebuds - getting a little more complex but manageable for a beginner with patience.

 Four Rosebuds - several stages building on top of one another. Each stage is straightforward, but there are more of them to follow or there may be several thread ends to manage.

Essential Ingredients

The simplest of supplies can make the most inspiring, beautiful and gorgeous designs. This is a quick guide to some of the bead types and materials used in this book. Most importantly; choose quality supplies and use colours that you love.

Seed Beads

Whether they are strung simply, or woven into leaves, flowers, flexible ropes or butterfly wings, seed beads feature in most of these designs.

The size of the seed bead is denoted as 15/0, 11/0, 10/0, 8/0 etc. - the larger the number, the smaller the bead will be. This book uses mainly sizes 15/0, 10/0, 8/0 and 6/0.

For fine detail, delicate petals and tiny bumble bee wings you will need size 15/0 seed beads.

Size 10/0 seed beads create stylised leaves, stems and tassel strands.

Size 8/0 and 6/0 seed beads, having larger holes, support petals and punctuate ropes where extra thread passes might be needed.

Choosing Your Seed Beads

High quality seed beads are manufactured in the Czech Republic and Japan. Czech seed beads tend to be a more rounded shape than the Japanese seed beads so they don't always work well together in a closely-woven piece. However these designs mix and match seed beads from both sources - they are just used for different purposes or within separate areas of the work.

All the size 10/0, 8/0 and 6/0 seed beads used in this book are of Czech manufacture, and the size 15/0 seeds are made by Miyuki in Japan. If you prefer you can use all of one manufacture, or the other.

Bugle Beads

Bugles are small glass tubes which are available in several lengths. You will need size 3 bugles, which are approximately 8mm long, for the Nocturne project.

Beading Needles & Beadwork Necessities

Beading needles have a very slim eye so they can pass through a bead with a small hole.
Size 10 Beading is a general beading needle that is suitable for straight stringing and simple weaving.
Size 13 Beading is a little finer for multiple passes of the thread through the bead holes and when working with smaller seed beads.

Sharp Scissors are essential to trim the threads close.

A Thread Conditioner such as Thread Heaven helps to smooth the kinks in the thread if you get into a knot or tangle.

A Fleece Bead Mat with a slight pile will stop the beads from rolling around and make it easy to pick up small beads with the point of the needle.

Clear Nail Polish or a clear fast-drying glue can be useful to seal the knots when the beadwork is complete.

Delica Beads

These are tiny cylinder-shaped glass beads used for accurate weaving as they will sit close together like bricks in a wall. Manufactured by Miyuki in Japan, they are available in several sizes and hundreds of colours. This book uses only size 11/0 Delicas.

Beading Thread

Sold under many brand names such as Nymo and Superlon, beading thread is available in several thicknesses and many colours. These projects all use a size D thread.

Twin Beads

With two parallel holes and a tapered profile, Twin beads are very versatile making tiny daisy motifs and structural components.

Knitted Tubular Wire

Knitted from 0.1mm wire this material is flexible, surprisingly strong and very versatile. Supplied flat-packed or on spools, it is available in a choice of widths and many colours. You will need 85mm diameter tubing for the Bouquet Necklace.

Findings

You will need just a few simple findings to complete some of the projects.

Jump rings are used for linking - soldered jump rings are particularly useful. Earfittings complete the earring designs.

Lapel pins and hat pins can be converted into beautiful brooches. Make sure you also have a pin guard for the end.

Fine stranded wire beading thread will be needed for the Honey Bee Earrings and 0.8mm plated wire to stiffen the centre of the Kyoto Necklace.

Fire Polished Faceted Glass

Sparkling glass beads with a smooth generous hole are extremely useful for flower centres, adding weight to fringe strands and linking different design elements together.

Crystal Beads

Precision cut from very high quality lead crystal glass these faceted beads give a maximum amount of sparkle.

Crystal beads are available in many shapes and sizes - this book uses faceted rounds & rondelles.

There are a few basic techniques that you will need to work through the projects in this book. If you need a special technique for a particular project it will be explained within that chapter but for the techniques that apply to most of the designs this is what you need to read.

Using a Keeper Bead

Before you start a piece of beadwork you will need to put a stopper at the end of the thread. The easiest stopper to use is a keeper bead.

A keeper bead is a spare bead, ideally of a different colour to the work, that is held on a temporary knot close to the end of the thread. Once the beading is completed the keeper bead is removed. That end of the thread is then secured and finished neatly within the beadwork.

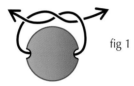

fig 1

To Add a Keeper Bead - Position the keeper bead 15cm from the end of the thread (unless instructed otherwise) and tie a simple overhand knot about the bead (fig 1). When you thread on the first beads of the pattern push them right up to the keeper bead - this tension in the thread will prevent the keeper bead from slipping.

When the work is complete, or the instructions say to do so, untie the knot and remove the keeper bead. Attach the needle to this end of the thread and finish off securely.

Correcting a Mistake

If you make a mistake whilst you are following a pattern remove the needle and pull the thread back until you have undone the work sufficiently. Do not turn the needle and try to pass it back through the holes in the beads - the needle tip will certainly catch another thread inside the beads and make a filamentous knot that is almost impossible to undo successfully.

Knotty Problems & Too Many Threads

When you are beadweaving the needle has to pass through the beads of the pattern many times.

Each time you pass through a bead the hole becomes a little more filled with thread. This can be used to advantage, as the beadwork will stiffen a little more with each extra thread pass. The extra firmness helps petals to hold their form, reinforces edges which need to support tassel strands and stops beaded wings from curling inwards.
However, as you continue to pass through the same beads, the holes become very congested.

If you need to continue to pass the needle through these congested beads you can swap to a finer needle or you may be able to find an alternative route through some adjacent beads. Do not force a needle through a blocked bead - you will probably break the bead and spoil the work.

The worst culprit for blocking holes in beads is a misplaced knot. If you must tie a knot before the beadwork is complete, take care to position it away from any future thread path. In many of the projects you will be asked to leave a thread end hanging loose and unfinished, whilst you continue with the pattern, to prevent the holes from becoming blocked. You will be instructed when to finish off these thread ends.

Following A Pattern & Help with Bead Recipes

Read through the project before you start. It will give you an overall view of 'what goes where' and why the stages are arranged in a particular order.

Some of the materials lists at the start of the projects are quite long. This makes for an interesting combination of colours or textures in the finished project but it can be a little confusing when you first start.

Make yourself a slim cardboard bookmark listing the beads A-Z with your own description of the colours and sizes, or even better, sew a few beads alongside the letters for a quick and accurate key to your bead palette.

Starting a New Thread & Finishing off a Thread End

You will need to add in new thread lengths when required and finish off unwanted thread ends neatly and securely.

Starting a New Thread

It is important that you do not block the holes in the beads with knots before the beadwork is complete. You may need to pass the needle through the current thread path several more times before the work is complete. Wherever possible the new thread is joined into the work using a keeper bead to avoid making any knots.

Work the old thread until you have no less than 15cm of length remaining. Remove the needle from this thread end and leave the end hanging loose. Prepare the needle with a new thread and tie a keeper bead 15cm from the end.

fig 2
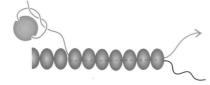

Starting 6-8 beads back from the old thread end pass the needle through the beadwork to emerge alongside the old thread end (fig 2). Pull the new keeper bead up snugly to the beadwork surface.

Continue with the pattern as before.
When the beadwork in that area is completely finished, or when instructed to do so, return to the thread ends and secure them using concealed knots (see below).

Finishing A Thread End

If necessary remove the keeper bead and attach the needle to the thread end.

Pass the needle through a few beads of the pattern. At that position pick up the thread between the beads with the point of the needle. Pull the needle through to leave a loop of thread 2cm in diameter. Pass the needle through the loop twice (fig 3) and gently pull down to form a concealed double knot between the beads.

fig 3

Pass the needle through five or six beads of the pattern and repeat the double knot.

Pass the needle through five or six more beads before trimming the thread end as close as possible to the work.

Making a Clasp with a Bead & Loop

The necklace and bracelet designs in this book are fastened with a bead and loop clasp. This type of clasp is simple to make, easy to use and minimises the number of materials you need to complete the design.

There is a Bead Tag on one side of the closure and a Bead Loop on the other. The typical combination of tag and loop will add up to 20mm to the finished length of your design.

The Bead Tag - A simple combination of seed beads for flexibility, and one or two larger beads to engage with the bead loop, this side of the clasp is normally made first and should be on the right of the necklace as worn.

The tag beads are added to the end of the design, an anchor is created, using one or three seed beads, and the needle passed back through the tag beads into the body of the design (fig 4).

A three seed bead anchor is more decorative than a single anchor bead.

For an adjustable clasp use two larger beads on the tag.

fig 4

The Bead Loop - For ease of use the bead loop is usually made from smaller, size 10/0 or 11/0, seed beads. The loop is made second so you can check it for size against the larger beads of the tag (fig 5).

fig 5

The loop should just fit over the larger tag beads. You need to check that the suggested bead count is correct for your work. The tag bead should just pop through the bead loop, don't make the loop too tight or you will place the thread under stress each time you use it.

Both the bead loop and the bead tag should be reinforced with one or more extra passes of thread.

Single or Doubled Thread

Most of the beadwork is made with a single thickness of beading thread.

The thread will build up through the beads as the pattern evolves - if extra strength or rigidity is required the needle can be passed through those beads two or three times.

A doubled thread is recommended for stringing, or when you need to attach larger, heavier beads such as the lucite flowers in the Bouquet Necklace (page 63).

Brick stitch is used in the Kyoto and Papillon Chapters. If you have not used this technique before it is a good idea to make a sampler ten beads x ten rows just to familiarise yourself with how the stitch works. Try out an increase and a decrease too so you are prepared to follow the pattern accurately.

Brick stitch is so called because of the pattern the beads form as they line up, in staggered rows, giving the impression of a brick wall. It can form flat pieces or tubes but both require a starter row or 'foundation row' on which the first row of brick stitch is worked.

1 The Ladder Stitch Foundation Row - This ladder of beads is worked so that all the holes of the beads are lined up perpendicular to the length of the row.

Prepare the needle with 1.5m of single thread and tie a keeper bead 15cm from the end. Thread on two beads. Pass the needle back down through the first bead and up through the second to bring the two beads alongside one another (fig 1).

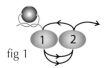
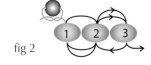

2 Thread on a third bead; pass the needle back up bead 2 and back down bead 3 (fig 2) bringing bead 3 to sit alongside beads 1 and 2. Repeat for seven further beads to give you a row of ten (fig 3).

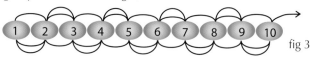

3 Starting to Brick Stitch - Thread on two beads (11 & 12). Pick up the loop of thread between beads 10 and 9 and pass back up through bead 12 in the opposite direction (fig 4). This should bring the two new beads to sit alongside one another with bead 11 slightly overhanging the previous row.

4 Thread on bead 13. Pick up the loop of thread between beads 9 and 8 and pass back up bead 13 (fig 5). Repeat adding one bead at a time to the end of the row (ten beads in total).

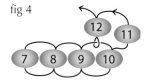
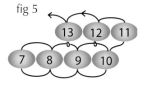

5 Pick up beads 21 and 22 to start the next row (fig 6) and work to the end of the row. Continue to work a further seven rows.

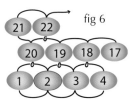

Each row starts with a two bead stitch followed by eight single bead stitches. The beads of each row should sit right alongside one another and the rows should sit closely on top of one another. You should not be able to see the thread except at the top and bottom of the work.

You will also need to know how to shape the work by increasing and decreasing the length of the rows.

6 Decreasing at the Start of the Row - A plain brick stitch row starts with a two-bead stitch. If you pick up the first loop of thread along the previous row, the new row will overhang by half of one bead (as fig 4). If you pick up the second loop along the new beads will sit half a bead in from the end of the previous row (fig 7) decreasing the row length by one bead.

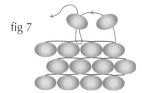

If you need to make a bigger decrease you can weave the needle up and down through the beads of the previous row until you are in the correct place to start the new row with a two-bead stitch (fig 8). The new two-bead stitch can stretch across two bead loops (as fig 7) if necessary, to follow the pattern correctly.

This method of repositioning the needle to start the beading in the correct position, with the needle pointing in the correct direction, to begin the stitch, is the main skill required to make a success of any brick stitch project.

7 Increasing at the End of the Row - Pick up one bead and pass the needle back up through the last bead of the row. Pass back down through the increase bead (fig 9) - this is just like making the foundation row.

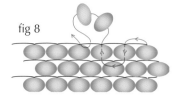

In fig 9 the needle is emerging in the wrong direction to start the next row from the newly increased bead. Pass the needle through the previous bead of this row and start the new row with a two-bead stitch from this bead - make sure you have picked out the correct two beads for this location on the pattern. You can then backtrack to add any beads required at the start of the row above the increase bead.

Herringbone Rope for Beginners

Herringbone Rope is used in several chapters: to make beautifully flexible and strong straps in the Sinensis Necklace and curving branches in the Kyoto Necklace. You will also find it used in a few Inspiration projects. If you have not used this technique before it is a good idea to make a twenty-row rope to familiarise yourself with the stitch.

Unusually for a beadwork stitch, Herringbone stitch adds two beads at a time. The two beads sit in a V or chevron. As the chevrons stack up into columns it resembles a herringbone patterned fabric. There are several methods for starting a Herringbone Rope. This one is quick to learn and has been successfully used to start the Herringbone Ropes in this book. If you are making a rope for the first time use two colours of seed beads, A and B, as this will help you to spot the end of a row.

figs show the work flat for clarity

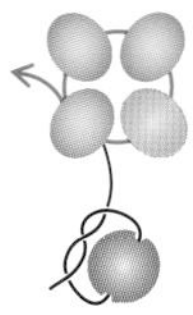

1 Prepare the needle with 1.2m of single thread and tie a keeper bead 15cm from the end. Thread on 3A and 1B. Pass through the first A bead to make a ring (fig 1).

fig 1

2 Thread on 2A.
Pass the needle through the next A bead to pull the new 2A into a chevron between the 2A on the ring (fig 2).
Pass through the next A of the ring and thread on 1A and 1B. Pass through the B bead of the ring to make a second chevron (fig 3).

fig 2

3 Pass through the next A of the ring and the first A of the first chevron. This completes the row and repositions the needle for the new row (fig 4).

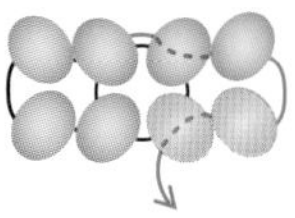

fig 3

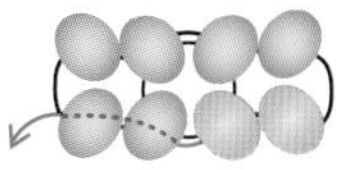

fig 4

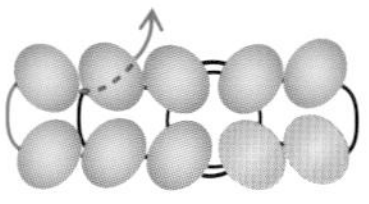

fig 5

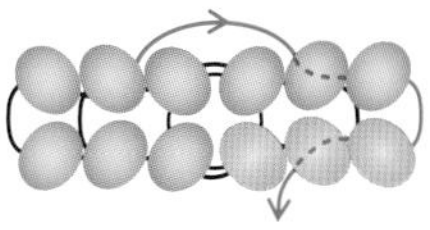

fig 6

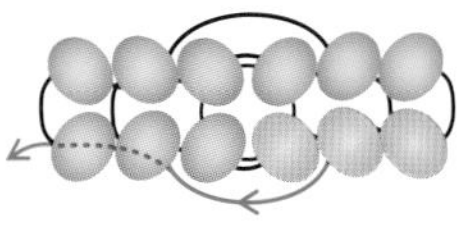

fig 7

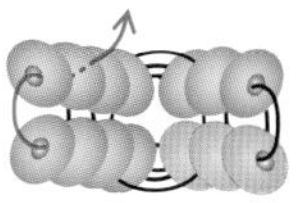

fig 8

4 Thread on 2A. Pass the needle through the next A to make a new chevron (fig 5).

Pass up through the A at the top of the next column. Thread on 1A and 1B. Pass through the next B (fig 6).
Finish the row by passing through the top 2A of the next column (fig 7).

Pull quite firmly on the thread to bring the two columns together into a little drum forming the end of the rope.

5 Start the new row with a 2A stitch (fig 8). Complete the row with a 1A, 1B stitch and pass up the first 2A of the first column. This is Herringbone Rope.

Continue with the same bead sequence. The rope will have a single row of B beads all the way along one edge.

Square Stitch for Beginners

Single Square Stitches are used throughout the projects to make links between motifs and links between rows of beads. Larger blocks of square stitch are used to make the leaves for the Daffodil Brooch.

A single square stitch passes the needle through one or two beads of the original row. It passes in the opposite direction through the same number of parallel beads and back through the original beads to make a square path with the thread (fig 1).

However a single square stitch can also be used to link beads of different sizes (fig 2) or to link two beads to one bead (fig 3).

The thread path is often far from 'square' but the holes in the linked beads are parallel.

The single square stitch is often repeated to make the link stronger.

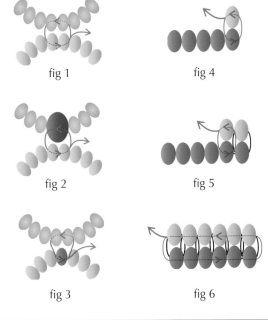

fig 1

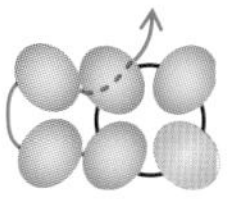

fig 2

fig 3

fig 4

fig 5

fig 6

A block of square stitch starts with a single row of beads.

A new bead is threaded for the start of the new row. This bead is square stitched to the last bead of the first row - the needle should finish pointing back along the first row (fig 4).

A second bead is added and square stitched to the next bead along the first row (fig 5).

This is repeated to the end of the row.

Before the needle is turned for the next row it should be passed up and down the two rows just worked to bring the beads neatly into line (fig 6).

Using Flower & Leaf Beads

A quick and easy way to making gorgeous floral designs
is to use flower and leaf-shaped beads.

Flower & leaf beads can be threaded, stitched, stacked and dangled.

Mix and match them with seed beads and simple beadwork motifs to make unique and exciting designs.

Flowers and leaves are some of the most commonly available fancy beads.

You will find beads made from glass, plastic, wood and metal in a multitude of colours and finishes.

Gorgeous Fuchsia Earrings can be yours in minutes.

Dangle three beaded headpin stamens from a looped pin.
Thread on an 8mm bead for the throat of the flower, a 28mm clematis flower bead and a 6mm pearl. Trim and loop the pin. Add the earfitting.

The addition of a couple of lucite leaf beads transforms dangling red hearts into juicy cherry earrings.

Choosing the Right Beads for Your Design

The direction of the hole in any leaf or flower bead is very important in the construction of your design.

The wrong bead in the wrong place may stick out awkwardly, lie sideways when you need it to dangle downwards or only show the thin edge to the front.

However, if you adapt your stringing method to include small anchor beads for flower centres and loops to support dangling leaves, your design options suddenly become endless.

Through-Hole

Pass down through the hole, thread on a seed bead anchor and pass up through the hole. Use this method to secure a stack of beads to make a more complex motif.

Top-Hole front-to-back

Thread on six seed beads. Pass through the hole in the leaf and thread on five seed beads. Pass through the first seed bead of the sequence.

Top-Hole side-to-side

These are easily added to a straight strung necklace or bracelet design. If you want them to dangle from the bottom of a strand make a loop.

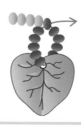

Fiji Necklace

This vibrant design combines both glass and lucite leaves and flowers.

A simple palette of two seed beads - green for the stringing and yellow for the flower centres brings the scheme together.

Small through-hole flower beads with seed bead centres form tight clusters along the front of the design.

The centre-front section, which supports the clusters, is made as a separate unit.

When the central section is complete, the side strings are added to make the necklace up to the desired length.

Threading Flower and Leaf Beads

If possible use a doubled beading thread if you are going to add glass flowers and leaves, which can be heavy, or larger lucite beads, which may catch and put strain on the thread.

If you prefer to use a single thread pass the needle back along the main strand supporting the fancy beads, to strengthen before you finish the design.

Adding Flower & Leaf Beads to Your Design

Start with a relatively plain row of seed beads - size 8/0 is ideal as these will have large holes to allow the thread to pass several times. You'll obviously need to include any spacer beads such as the plain rounds on the Violet Necklace (right).

Pass the needle back through the first strand to emerge at the correct position for the first leaf or flower.

To Add a Through-Hole Flower - Thread on the flower and a seed bead for the centre. Pass back through the flower and the previous seed bead on the first strand (fig 1). This centres the back of the flower on this seed bead and stops the thread along the first strand from distorting.

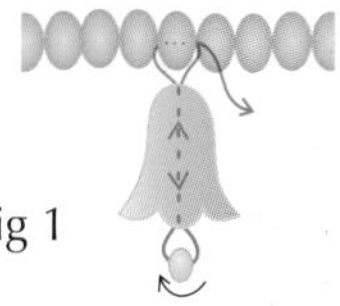

fig 1

To Add a Flower and Leaf Stack - Thread on the leaf and flower combination and the seed bead for the centre. As with the single flower pass back through the stack and the previous seed bead on the first strand (fig 2).

If the needle will fit through the beads again pass it back up and down the stack and through the seed bead on the first strand again.

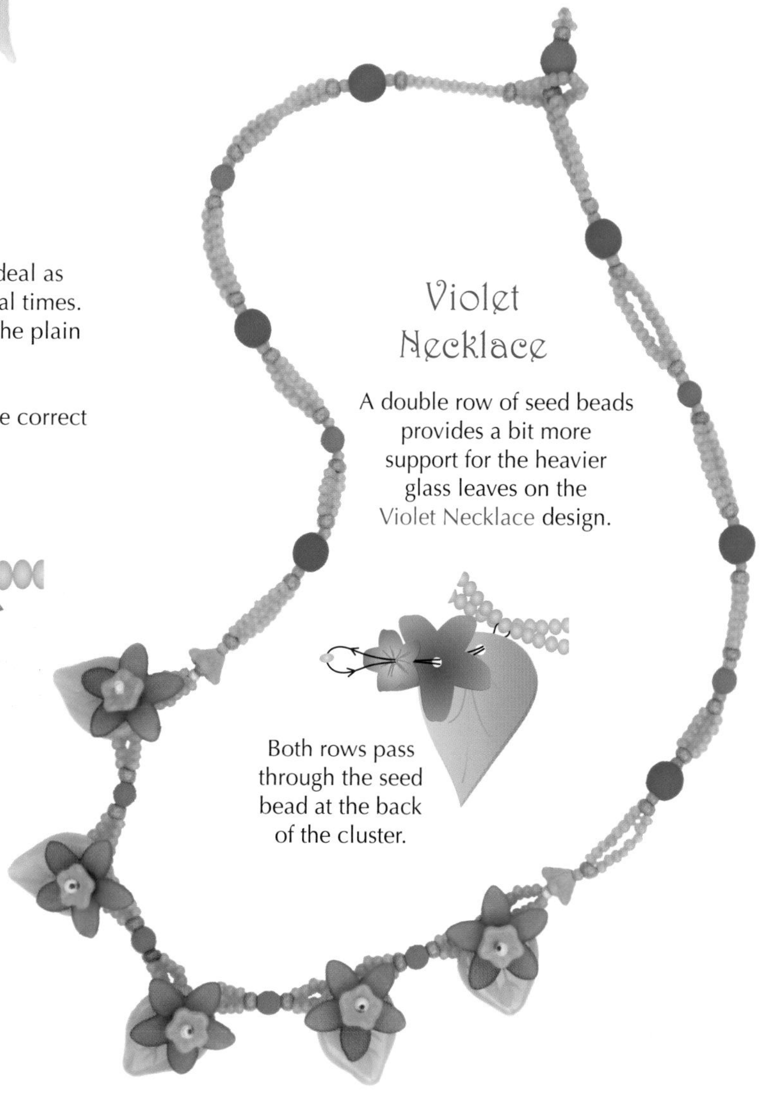

fig 2

Violet Necklace

A double row of seed beads provides a bit more support for the heavier glass leaves on the Violet Necklace design.

Both rows pass through the seed bead at the back of the cluster.

These two necklaces are made in size 10/0 seed beads.

Weaving Simple Motifs

A few seed beads quickly transform into simple leaf motifs.

Add Twin beads or Pip beads to your list of ingredients and you can smother your designs with perfect little daisies too.

Leaves with a Central Vein

Thread on sufficient S beads to reach the first leaf position. Thread on 1S and 11L.

Leaving aside the last 3L beads to anchor the strand pass back up the first 8L (fig 5).

Thread on 10L and pass the needle through the 3L of the anchor (fig 6).

Thread on 10L. Pass the needle down through the 8L of the central vein (fig 7).

fig 5

fig 6

fig 7

Pass the needle through the 3L of the anchor, up the 8L of the central vein and the single S above the leaf.

Pass the needle through the previous S on the main string to centralise the leaf (fig 8).

fig 8

Key
L - Leaf colour seed beads
S - Stringing seed beads

Simple Leaves

A simple leaf outline is very quick to make.

Thread on sufficient S beads to reach the first leaf position. Thread on 9L. Pass the needle back up through the eighth L bead to make the leaf tip (fig 1).

fig 1

Thread on 6L and pass through the very first L bead in the same direction (fig 2). This last stitch opens out the top of the loop to create the leaf profile.

fig 2

Note the second edge of the leaf uses three beads less than the first count.

Thread on a few S beads and repeat (fig 3).

fig 3

To Make a Larger Leaf -
Thread on more L beads for the first leaf edge. Make the leaf tip as before.

Thread on four beads less than the first edge bead count and pass through the first two L beads of the leaf sequence (fig 4).

fig 4

Passing through two beads, rather than one as before, opens out the leaf loop a little further to create a wider profile.

Seed bead leaves and Twin bead daisies make a perfect summer bracelet.

14

Twin Bead Daisies

These little daisy motifs sit very well along a single string of seed beads. You will need a small seed bead for the daisy centre too - a size 10/0 or 11/0 seed bead is ideal.

Twin beads have two parallel holes. It is important that you pass through the same hole on each bead when making these daisies.

Making a Daisy - Thread on six Twin beads.

Pass the needle through the same hole on the first Twin bead to make a ring (fig 9).

fig 9

Pass the needle through all the beads of the ring again to make it firm - make sure you pass through the same hole on each bead.

Thread on a seed bead for the daisy centre. Pass the needle through the Twin bead on the opposite side of the ring.

Pass back through the centre seed bead and the first Twin bead again in the same direction - the thread has made a figure of eight (fig 10).

fig 10

Pass through the next Twin bead of the ring.

fig 11

Flip the daisy over so you are looking at the reverse of the motif. Add a seed bead to the centre of the motif on this side - make sure you pass through the opposite Twin bead so the seed bead sits centrally (fig 11). This second central seed bead makes the daisy reversible and stronger too.

Pass the needle through the next two Twin beads to emerge three petals around from the main string (fig 12).

fig 12

You can now continue with the stringing for your design.

Making Flowers with Pip Beads on a Seed Bead Strand

Slightly larger than the Twin beads, the Pip bead flowers on the Alison Necklace design are made with a similar method.

Thread on six Pip beads. Pass through the holes in the six Pip beads again to make a ring (fig 13).

Thread on a 4mm round bead and pass through the third Pip bead around the ring in the opposite direction to make the centre of the flower (fig 14).

Don't add a 4mm centre bead to the back of the flower - it will be too bulky to allow the motif to lie flat.

Continue with the main string of your design.

fig 13

fig 14

fig 15

Each flower on the Alison Necklace is made from six petal-shaped beads.

The petal-shaped beads are called 'Pip beads' and have a side-to-side top hole.

When the main string is complete pass the needle back through the seed bead row to emerge behind the last Pip bead flower. Thread on two or three seed beads to bridge the central gap across the back of the flower and pass through the next section of seed bead stringing (fig 15). Repeat to the end of the row.

Carmen Necklace
& Bracelet

necklace measures 43cm
bracelet measures   20cm

Graduated

flowers in soft, sun-bleached tones make a delightful central feature in this summery necklace design. These motifs are so versatile - they easily adapt to make a matching bracelet.
Try frosty white and sparkling grey for a sophisticated evening outfit or tropical brights for a holiday in the sun.

You Will Need

To Make the Necklace

10g of size 10/0 silver lined eau de Nil seed beads A
5g of size 10/0 silver lined lilac seed beads B
3g of size 6/0 silver lined frost purple AB seed beads C
Thirty-nine 4mm olive AB fire polished faceted beads D
Two 6mm olive AB fire polished faceted beads E
Two 6mm purple AB fire polished faceted beads F
Ash-colour size D beading thread

To Make the Bracelet

5g of size 10/0 silver lined eau de Nil seed beads A
5g of size 10/0 silver lined lilac seed beads B
3g of size 6/0 silver lined frost purple AB seed beads C
Forty 4mm olive AB fire polished faceted beads D
Two 6mm purple AB fire polished faceted beads F
Ash-colour size D beading thread

Tools

A size 10 beading needle
A pair of scissors to trim the threads

The Necklace is Made in Five Stages

The central flower with seven petals is made first.
Followed by two flowers with six petals each.
Four flowers with five petals complete the set.
The flowers are linked together to make the centrepiece.
The side straps are added to finish the design.

1 The Seven-Petal Flower - Prepare the needle with 1.5m of single thread and tie a keeper bead 15cm from the end.

Thread on 14A. Pass the needle through the first A bead once more to bring the beads into a ring (fig 1).

Pass the needle through the 14A beads once more to make the circle a little more firm.

fig 1

2 Thread on 1A, 1C and 1A.

Pass the needle through the two previous A beads on the ring and the following 2A beads of the ring (fig 2).

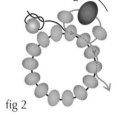

fig 2

3 Thread on 1A and 1C.

Referring to fig 3 pass the needle through the first A bead of the previous stitch, the last 2A beads passed through on the ring and the following 2A beads of the ring.

Repeat step 3 four more times.

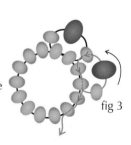

fig 3

4 Pass the needle up through the second A bead added in step 2 and thread on 1C.

Pass the needle down through the first A bead of the previous stitch, the following 2A beads of the ring and the first A bead passed through on this stitch once more. This adds the last C bead of the sequence and repositions the needle for the next step (fig 4).

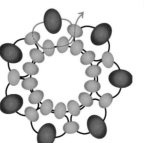

fig 4

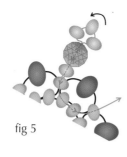 Thread on 1B, 1D and 3B.

Leaving aside the last 3B beads threaded to anchor the strand, pass the needle back through the D bead and the following 1B and 1A.

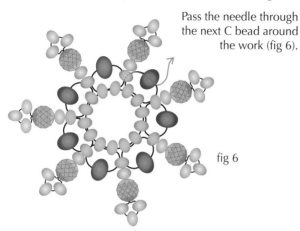

fig 5

Pass the needle through the following 2A beads of the ring and the A bead between the next 2C beads along to emerge at the edge of the beading (fig 5).

Repeat from the beginning of step 5 six times to add a total of seven D bead spikes around the circle (see fig 6).

Pass the needle through the next C bead around the work (fig 6).

fig 6

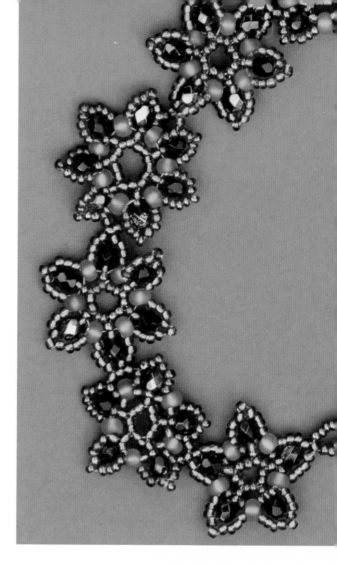

Thread on 3B. Pass the needle through the 3B beads of the anchor on the following spike and thread on 3B. Pass the needle through the following 1C bead (fig 7).

Repeat step 6 six more times to complete the petals.

The petals now need to be reinforced.

fig 7

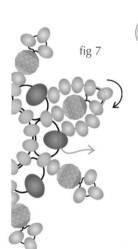

The Six-Petal Flower - On this flower the A and B beads swap over to reverse the colours.

Prepare the needle as before. Thread on 12B and make into a ring as in step 1.

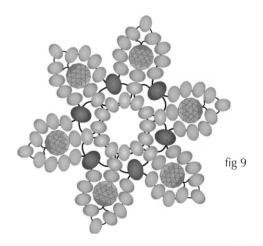

fig 9

fig 8

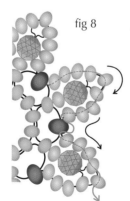

Referring to fig 8 pass the needle through the 9B beads around the edge of the first petal.

Skip the following C bead and pass up through the B beads of the next petal (fig 8).

Work all around the flower passing the needle through the B beads of the petal edges and skipping the C beads - this will make the flower a little more firm.

Leave the thread ends attached but remove the needle. Set aside for the moment.

You now have six sets of two beads to support the petals, rather than the seven sets of two beads, in the seven-petal flower instructions.

Make the six-petal flower with the same technique as the seven-petal flower replacing the A beads with B beads and vice versa (fig 9).

Repeat to make a second identical flower.

9 The Five-Petal Flower - Prepare the needle as before and thread on 10A. Make into a ring as in step 1.

This ring of beads is quite small so the thread for the next row will follow a tighter curve as you add the C beads. Two extra beads are added to each stitch to prevent the thread pulling too tight and distorting the flower.

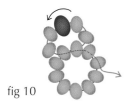

fig 10

10 Thread on 2A, 1C and 2A.

Pass the needle through the previous 2A beads of the ring and the following 2A as before (fig 10).

Thread on 2A, 1C and 1A.

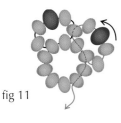

fig 11

11 Pass the needle through the first A bead of the previous stitch and the following 4A beads of the ring as before (fig 11).

Repeat step 11 twice.

12 For the last stitch around the ring pass the needle up through the fourth A bead of the first petal and thread on 1A, 1C and 1A.

Pass the needle down the first A bead of the last petal and the following 2A of the ring and 1A between the C beads (fig 12).

You are now in the correct position to add the first petal.

Add the petals as before in B and D beads working from step 5 to the end of step 6.

fig 12

To reinforce the petals pass the needle through the outer beads of the flower once more - this time pass through the C beads instead of skipping past them or the flower may distort.

Leave the thread ends attached and remove the needle.

Make one more five-petal flower to match.
Make two more five-petal flowers replacing the A beads with B beads and vice versa (fig 13).

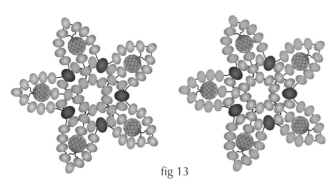

fig 13

Make two of these   Make two of these

---

13 Linking the Flowers - Fig 14 shows the shape and colour arrangement of the finished centrepiece.

fig 14

Note that the colours alternate.

The seven-petal flower in the centre shows a central petal on the top edge of the design.

The two six-petal flowers show two petals on the top edge.

The first two five-petal flowers show two petals on the top edge and the last five-petal flower on side edge shows the remainder of the necklace length attaching to the second petal.

Refer back to this diagram as you make the links.

> ## Extra Info....
> When you reposition the needle through the beadwork make sure you follow an existing thread path - if you skip across a gap, however small, you may cause the work to distort.

14 The first link is between the seven-petal flower and the first of the six-petal flowers.

Referring to fig 14 you will see that the petal tip of the six-petal flower fits into the V-shape between the petals on the seven-petal flower.

Attach the needle to the longest thread end on the six-petal flower.

Pass through the beads of the six-petal flower to emerge from the A bead at the tip of one of the petals.

fig 15

15 Thread on 1A. Referring to fig 15, pass the needle through the 2B before the C bead, the C bead and the following 2B beads on the seven-petal flower.

Thread on 1A and pass the needle through the A bead at the tip of the six-petal flower (fig 15).

Pass the needle through the beads of the link once more to reinforce the join.

16 Pass the needle through the beads of the six-petal flower to emerge from the A bead at the tip of the opposite petal ready to attach to the next flower along (the first-five petal flower as shown in fig 14).

This petal attaches to the V in the first five-petal flower in exactly the same way. Make the link and finish off the thread neatly and securely.

17 Pick up the last five-petal flower on this side of the design. Referring to fig 14 the tip of a petal on this flower attaches in the V-shape of the previous five-petal flower.

Attach the needle to the longest thread end on the new five-petal flower and pass the needle through to emerge from the A bead at the tip of one of the petals.

Lay the work down in front of you so you can orientate the flower correctly with the links already made. Double check with fig 14 and make the link as in fig 15.

Once the link is reinforced with a second pass of the thread finish off the thread neatly and securely.

Repeat from step 14 to join the remaining flower motifs to the other side of the centrepiece.

18 The Side Straps - Prepare the needle with 1.5m of single thread and tie a keeper bead 15 cm from the end.

Thread on 1C, 1A, 1B, 1E, 1B, 1A, 1C, 1A and 6B.

Referring to fig 14 pass the needle through the A bead at the tip of the correct petal on the last five-petal flower on one side of the centrepiece.

Thread on 6B.

Pass the needle back up through the 1A, 1C, 1A, 1B, 1E, 1B, 1A and 1C beads to emerge alongside the keeper bead (fig 16).

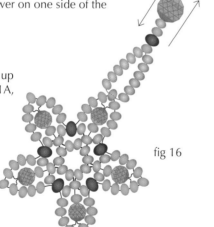

fig 16

19 Take a generous pinch of the A beads and mix together with a few B beads so you have 1B bead for approximately every 7 or 8 A beads. Use this mixture for the stringing.

Thread on sufficient of this stringing mix to reach the centre back of your necklace.

20 Thread on 1F, 1A, 1C, 1A, 1F, 1A and 3B.

Leaving aside the last 3B beads threaded to anchor the strand, pass the needle back down the last A bead threaded and the following five beads to emerge from the first F bead of the sequence (fig 17).

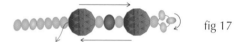

fig 17

Thread on the same length of stringing mix beads as before.

Pass the needle through the 1C, 1A, 1B, 1E, 1B, 1A, 1C, 1A and 6B just before the centrepiece of the necklace, the A bead at the tip of the petal and back through the following 6B, 1A, 1C, 1A, 1B, 1E, 1B, 1A and 1C beads to emerge alongside the keeper bead.

Reinforce the two straps with a second pass of the needle.

Remove the keeper beads and finish off the thread ends neatly and securely.

21 Start the strap at the other side of the design as in steps 18 and 19. You will need to add the looped side of the clasp.

Thread on 1C, 1A and 1B. Now thread on sufficient of the stringing mix to make a loop that will just fit over the E beads of the tag made in step 20 (approximately 17 beads).

Pass the needle back through the 1B, 1A and 1C beads to draw up the loop (fig 18).

fig 18

Complete the strap to match the other side of the design.

Remove any remaining keeper beads and finish off any loose threads neatly and securely.

Carmen Bracelet

The Bracelet is Made in Three Stages

The individual flowers are made first.
The flowers are linked together.
The bead and loop clasp is added.

22 Making the Flowers - Following steps 9 to 12 make three five-petal flowers in each colourway.

These six flowers will enable you to start the bracelet links.

Extra Info....
The six flower motifs made in step 22 will measure
14.5cm when linked together.
Each additional flower will add a further 2.5cm.
The clasp will add up to 2.5cm to the finished length.

With this information you can calculate how many
more flowers you will need to make
the perfect bracelet.

23 Making the Links - Fig 19 shows the pattern of the links along the length of the bracelet. You can see that the colours alternate and the flower motifs zigzag up and down.

fig 19

Fig 20 shows the beads that need to link together between two adjacent flowers.

Line up the edge of one flower to the edge of another with the sides of two petals touching where they overlap and compare them to fig 20.

You will link together the two beads shown in yellow, the two shown in pink and the two shown in blue.

fig 20

These bracelets measure 20cm
- see the Extra Info box for
more sizing information.

24 Attach the needle to the longest thread end on the first flower.

Pass through the beads of the motif to emerge from the bead coloured yellow in fig 20 with the needle pointing towards the tip of the petal.

Make a square stitch between this yellow-coloured bead and the yellow-coloured bead on the next flower motif along the sequence (fig 21).

Repeat the stitch to reinforce the join.

fig 21

25 Pass the needle through the adjacent bead indicated in pink on fig 20 and square stitch to the pink bead on the second flower (fig 22).

Reinforce with a second pass of the thread and move on to repeat with the beads indicated blue on fig 20.

Finish off the thread neatly and securely.

fig 22

Referring to fig 19 for the next placement, work along the length to join the first six flowers together.

Make and add more flowers as required to get a good fit.

26 The Clasp - If necessary add a new thread and bring it through to emerge from the C bead closest to one end of the bracelet.

Thread on 4B, 1A, 1F, 1A, 1C, 1A, 1F, 1A and 3B.

Leaving aside the last 3B beads to anchor the strand pass the needle back through the 1A, 1F, 1A, 1C, 1A ,1F and 1A beads.

Thread on 4B and pass the needle through the C bead at the end of the bracelet in the same direction as before (fig 23).

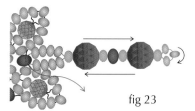

fig 23

Pass the needle through the beads just added for a second time to reinforce the tag and finish off the thread securely.

27 At the other end of the bracelet attach the needle to the longest thread end and pass through the motif to emerge from the corresponding C bead.

Thread on 4B, 1A, 1C, 1B and sufficient A beads to make a loop that will just fit over the F beads of the clasp tag made in step 26 (approximately 17A).

Pass the needle through the 1B, 1C and 1A beads to draw up the loop and thread on 4B.

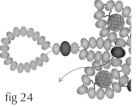

fig 24

Pass the needle through the C bead at the end of the bracelet in the same direction as before (fig 24).

Pass the needle through the beads just added to reinforce the work.

Finish off the thread and any remaining thread ends neatly and securely.

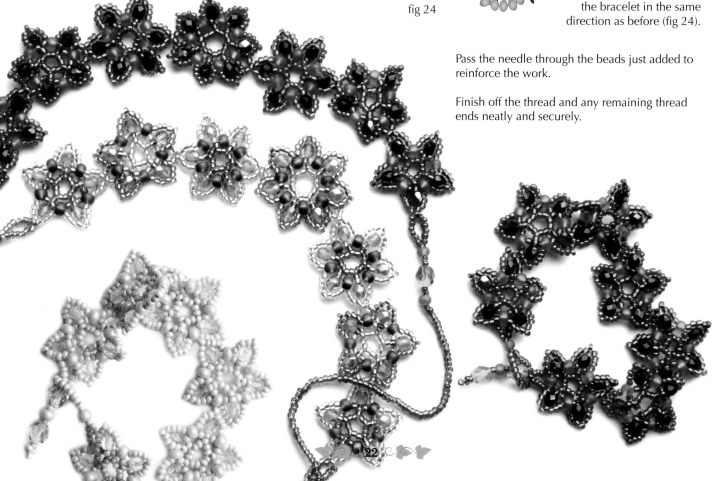

Mirabelle Necklace & Earrings

Based on the six-petal Carmen motif, this is an easy adaptation that changes the flowers into fluttering butterflies.

You Will Need

To Make the Necklace & Earrings

8g of size 10/0 opaque frost turquoise seed beads A
5g of size 10/0 metallic silver seed beads B
5g of size 6/0 metallic seed beads C
Seventy-nine 4mm matt opaque teal
fire polished faceted beads D
Three 6mm metallic silver fire polished faceted beads E
A pair of earfittings
Two 6mm jump rings
Turquoise size D beading thread

necklace measures 43cm

Mirabelle Necklace & Earrings

The Necklace is Made in Three Stages

The three butterfly motifs for the centrepiece are made first.
The fringe strands are added to the butterflies.
The side straps are added to complete the necklace.

28 The Butterflies - Referring to step 1 start with a ring of 2B and 10A. Finish with the needle emerging from the second A bead after the 2B (fig 25).

fig 25

Referring to step 2 thread on 1A, 1C and 1B and make the stitch (fig 26).

Referring to step 3 make three stitches with 1A and 1C.

Make the fourth stitch with 1B and 1C.

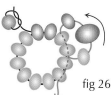

fig 26

Pass through the following 2A on the ring and the 1A in the gap ready to add the first D bead spike (fig 27).

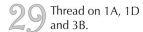

fig 27

30 Thread on 3B and pass through the 3B of the anchor. Thread on 3B and pass through the next C bead (fig 30). Repeat three times.

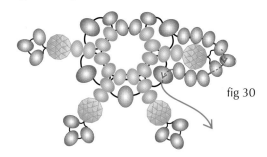

fig 30

29 Thread on 1A, 1D and 3B.

As in step 5 pass back down the D bead, the 2A below it, the following 2A of the ring and the 1A in the next gap (fig 28).

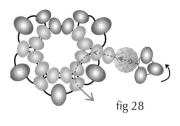

fig 28

31 Pass through the following 1B and thread on 1B.

Pass through the 2B on the ring and thread on 1B.

Pass through the following 1B (fig 31).

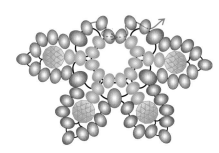

fig 31

Repeat to add a D bead spike in each of the next three gaps. Pass through the single B bead and the C bead ready to add the edging row (fig 29).

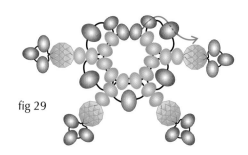

fig 29

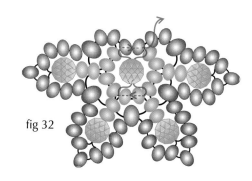

fig 32

Pass through all the B beads around the edge of the motif finishing at the 2B of the ring. Add 1D to the centre of the ring with a linking stitch between these 2B and the opposite 2A of the ring (fig 32).

You have completed the butterfly. Leave the thread ends attached and make two more motifs to match.

32 The Fringe Strands - Attach the needle to the longest thread end on the first motif. Fig 33 shows the positions for the fringe strands on the central motif.

 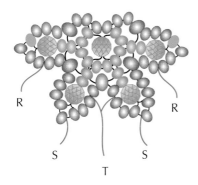

fig 33

R   R

S   S

T

Strand sequences -
R - 7A, 2B, 2A, 1C, 1A, 1B, 1D, 1B, 1A
S - 9A, 2B, 2A, 1C, 1A, 1B, 1D, 1B, 1A
T - 19A, 2B, 2A, 1C, 1A, 1B, 1D, 1B, 1A, 1E, 1A, 1B

 Reposition the needle to emerge at the first position R. Thread on the indicated beads. At the bottom of the strand leave aside the last bead to anchor the strand (fig 34) and pass the needle back up to the top of the strand Repeat at the first S position to make a slightly longer strand.

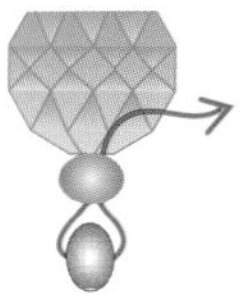

fig 34

33 The central strand at position T needs to bridge across the lower two 'wings' (see fig 33).

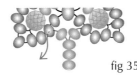

fig 35

Exit through one of the indicated T gaps in fig 33. Thread on the strand beads for position T and make the fringe strand anchor at the bottom as fig 34.

Pass up the strand beads to emerge 1A below the top of the sequence. Thread on 1A and pass through the second T gap on the wing edge (fig 35).

Complete the last two fringe strands at S and R as before.

34 The positions for the fringe strands for the two side motifs are shown in fig 36. You need to make one a mirror image of the other.

Use the longest thread on each motif to make the strands.

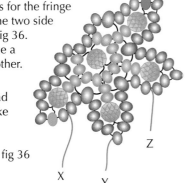

fig 36

Z

X   Y

Strand sequences -
X - 6A, 2B, 2A, 1C, 1A, 1B, 1D, 1B, 1A
Y - 4A, 1C, 1A, 1B, 1D, 1B, 1A
Z - 3A, 1C, 1A, 1B, 1D, 1B, 1A

35 When the strands are complete use the remaining thread ends to link the two side motifs to the central motif.

Use 1D bead for each link making a simple stitch between the beads marked orange in figs 33 and 36 (see fig 37).

Finish off the thread ends neatly and securely.

fig 37

36 The Side Straps - The side straps attach to the A beads marked green in fig 36.

With a new 80cm thread and keeper bead, thread on 1D. Pass through the indicated bead on fig 36 and back through the D bead just added.

Thread on 1B, 1A, 1C, 1A, 1B, 1D, 1B, 5A, 1B, 1A, 1C, 1A, 1B, 7A, 1B, 1D, 1B, 9A, 1B, 1A, 1C, 1A, 1B, 11A, 1B, 1D, 1B, 13A, 1B, 1A, 1C, 1A, 1B, 15A, 1B, 1D, 1B, followed by sufficient A beads to make the strap up to length.

37 Add a bead tag as in step 20 and pass back down the strand to the keeper bead, Finish off the thread ends neatly and securely.

Repeat at the other side adding a bead loop as in step 21 to complete the fastening.

The Mirabelle Earrings

38 Make two motifs. Following fig 33 for the strand positions make the strands with the combinations -

R - 3A, 2B, 1A, 1B, 1D, 1B and 1A
S - 4A, 2B, 1A, 1B, 1D, 1B and 1A
T - 11A, 2B, 1A, 1B, 1D, 1B and 1A

39 The triangular suspension strands attach to the top row of B beads one bead further in towards the centre than the orange beads on fig 33.

Starting at the correct position on the top edge, thread on 4A, 1B, 1D, 1B, 11A, 1D, 2A, 1C and 2A.

Pass back down the D bead to make a loop and thread on 11A, 1B, 1D, 1B and 4A. Attach to the opposite location.

Strengthen with a second pass of thread.

Finish off the thread ends neatly and securely.

Use a 6mm jump ring to link the earfitting to the C bead at the top of the design. Repeat to make the second earring.

Rosella Choker

This lustrous rosette of layered petals brings to mind late-summer Dahlias.

In the Carmen Necklace the flowers are designed to lie flat. Here we want texture and depth, so the petals are fitted tightly around three separate rings and cupped to stack, one just inside the other.

flower
diameter
5cm

You Will Need

5g of size 10/0 silver lined red seed beads A
2g of size 10/0 silver lined orange seed beads B
5g of size 6/0 transparent garnet AB seed beads C
8g of size 10/0 transparent garnet AB seed beads D
Five 4mm orange fire polished faceted beads E
Ten 4mm red fire polished faceted beads F
Eighteen 4mm garnet fire polished faceted beads G
One 6mm orange fire polished faceted bead H

50cm of 15mm wide black satin or grosgrain ribbon together with a suitable fastener such as a hook and eye, a press-stud or a Velcro tab

Red size D beading thread

The Choker is Made in Four Stages

The small flower is made first.
The medium flower is made second.
The large flower is made third.
The motifs are stacked, stitched together and a bar is added to the reverse to carry the ribbon.

40 The Small Flower - This flower has five petals and is worked in A, B, C and E beads.
Prepare the needle with 80cm of single thread and thread on 10A. Referring to step 1 bring them into a ring.

Following the techniques in steps 2, 3 and 4 add the A and C bead stitches. You will notice that the work is starting to cup.

41 Thread on 1A, 1E and 3B. Leaving aside the last 3B to anchor the strand pass back through the E bead and the following 2A.

Pass through the next 2A on the ring and the A bead between the next 2C (fig 38).

fig 38

fig 39

Repeat step 41 four times to make five spikes in total and pass the needle through the next C bead (fig 39).

42 Referring to step 6 add 3B ten times to complete the petal edges.

Referring to step 7 strengthen the petal edges with a second pass of thread - as you skip past the C beads the petals will pull up into a firmer, cupped profile.

Leave the threads attached, remove the needle and set aside for the moment.

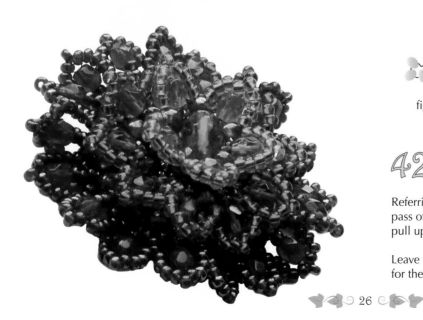

43 The Medium Flower - This flower has ten petals and is worked in A, C, D and F beads. Prepare the needle with 1.2m of single thread and thread on 20D. Referring to step 1 bring them into a ring.

Using D beads instead of A beads follow steps 2, 3 and 4.

44 Thread on 2D, 1F and 3A.

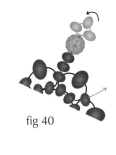

Leaving aside the last 3A to anchor the strand pass the needle back through the F bead and the following 3D.

Pass through the next 2D on the ring and the D bead between the next 2C (fig 40).

fig 40

Repeat step 44 nine times to complete ten spikes. Pass the needle through the next C bead (as fig 39).

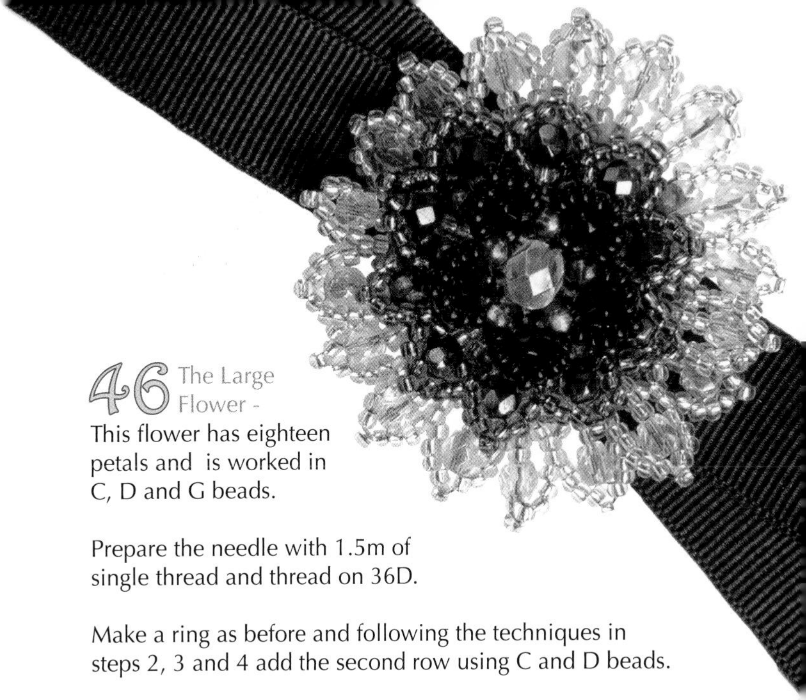

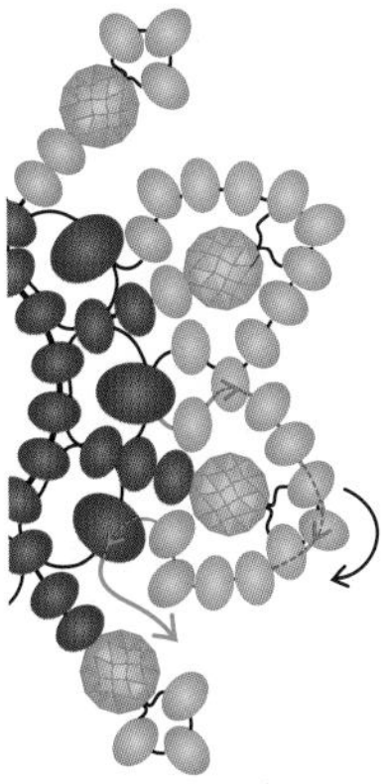

46 The Large Flower -
This flower has eighteen petals and is worked in C, D and G beads.

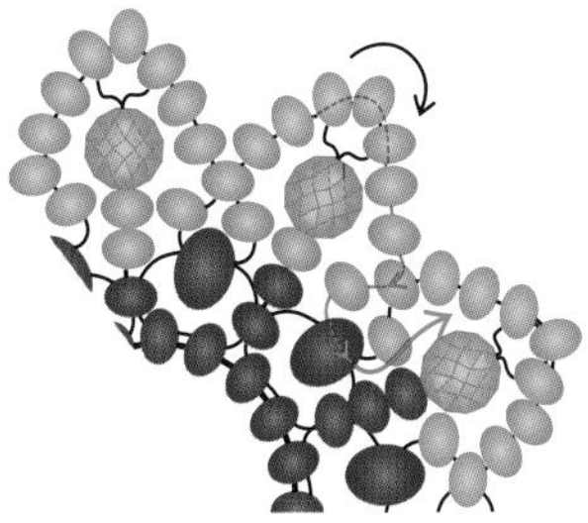

Prepare the needle with 1.5m of single thread and thread on 36D.

Make a ring as before and following the techniques in steps 2, 3 and 4 add the second row using C and D beads.

For each G bead spike thread on 5D, 1G and 3D. Repeat the technique in step 5 to make eighteen spikes in total.

Pass the needle through the next C bead (as fig 39).

45 Thread on 4A. Pass the needle through the 3A beads of the anchor and thread on 4A.

Pass through the next C bead (as in step 6).

Referring to fig 41 thread on 1A. Pass through the third A of the previous 4A and thread on 2A.

Pass through the next 3A anchor. Thread on 4A and pass through the next C.

Repeat the stitch shown in fig 41 seven times.

Start the last petal edge as for the previous petal and pass through the last 3A anchor.

Thread on 2A and pass down through the second A of the first 4A stitch. Thread on 1A and pass through the C bead (fig 42).

Leave the threads attached, remove the needle and set aside for the moment.

fig 41

fig 42

47 For the first petal edge thread on 6D. Pass through the anchor at the top of the spike and thread on 6D. Pass through the next C (as before).

Thread on 1A and pass up through the fifth and fourth D of the previous stitch. Thread on 3D and pass through the 3D anchor. Thread on 6D and pass through the next C bead (fig 43).

Repeat the stitch shown in fig 43 fifteen times.

Repeat once more linking the last side of the petal to the first 6A stitch.

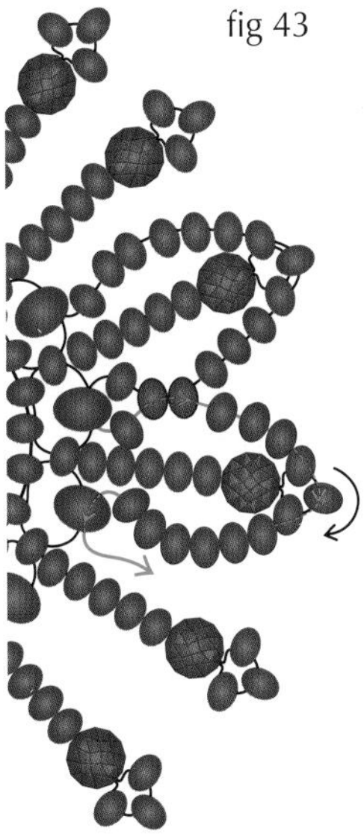

fig 43

48 Assembling the Design - Stack the flowers. Working from the reverse, use the closest available thread end to stitch the central ring of the small flower to the central ring of the medium flower - pull the thread firmly.

Stitch the inner ring of the large flower to the C beads of the middle flower - again pull firmly. Add the H bead to the centre of the stack pulling it firmly into the cup at the front.

Make two immediately adjacent parallel straps of 11D across the back of the large flower ring to create a channel for the ribbon. Square stitch these two rows together to make a firm band.

Finish off all the thread ends neatly and securely.

Thread the ribbon through the channel and finish off the ribbon ends to size with your chosen fastening method.

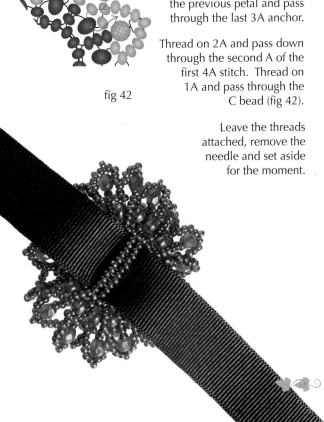

Daffodil Brooch

You Will Need

To Make the Yellow Pin

2.5g of DB0053 pale yellow lined Delica beads A
3g of DB0689 semi-matt pale grey-green Delica beads B
One 3mm topaz fire polished faceted bead C
Two 4mm topaz fire polished faceted beads D
One 4mm soldered jump ring
One 50mm gilt headpin
One 75mm gilt lapel pin with a flat head
One pin guard to match the lapel pin
One gilt French crimp
White size D beading thread

To Make the White & Yellow Pin

Replace the A beads above with -
1g of DB0053 pale yellow lined Delica beads A
1.5g of DB0201 ceylon white Delica beads E

all other materials remain the same as above

Tools

A size 10 beading needle
A pair of scissors to trim the threads
A pair of flat-faced pliers

The finished motif is 35mm across and 55mm tall
- the pin adds a further 45mm to the length

Gorgeous

yellow, apricot and burnt orange trumpets burst out from the cold winter soil to proclaim the arrival of the Spring.

This single-stemmed brooch makes a perfect gift for Easter.

The Brooch is Made in Five Stages

The five flat petals at the back of the flower are made first.
The trumpet is added to the centre of the flat petals.
The leaves are made separately.
The flower and the leaves are assembled to form a spray.
The lapel pin is added to complete the brooch.

Extra Info....
If you want to make the white and yellow brooch work steps 1 to 9 using the E beads.

1 The Flat Petals - Prepare the needle with 1.5m of single thread and tie a keeper bead 15cm from the end.

Thread on 10A.

Pass the needle through the first 1A of the 10A once more to bring the beads into a circle (fig 1).

These ten beads will support the five petals - two beads for the base of each petal.

fig 1

2 Thread on 12A.

Leaving aside the last 3A beads to anchor the strand pass the needle back down the previous 9A to make a spike of A beads.

Referring to fig 2 pass the needle through the previous A bead on the ring and the A bead where the needle emerged (fig 2).

Tension the thread so the two A beads on the ring support the spike equally.

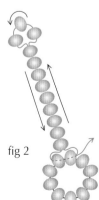

fig 2

3 Thread on 10A.
Pass the needle through the 3A beads of the anchor at the end of the spike (fig 3).

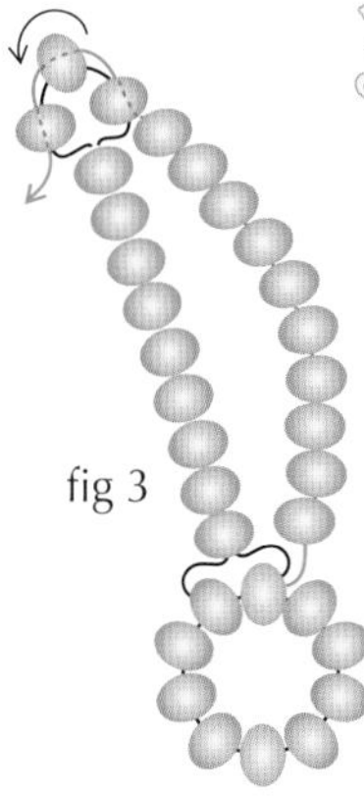

Thread on 10A and pass the needle through the 2A beads on the ring that support the petal (fig 4).

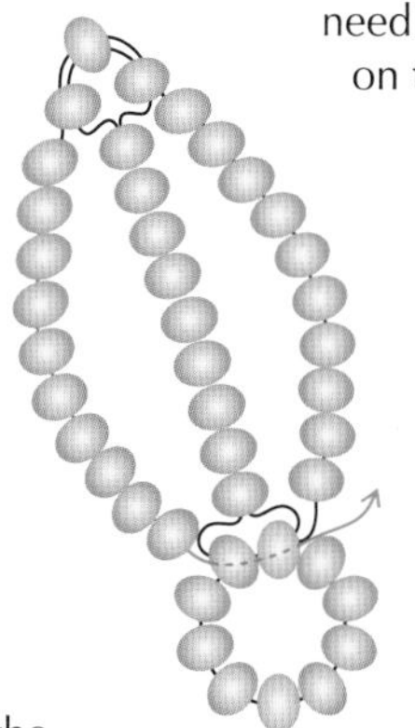

fig 3

fig 4

4 Pass the needle up through the first 7A of the first side of the petal (fig 5).

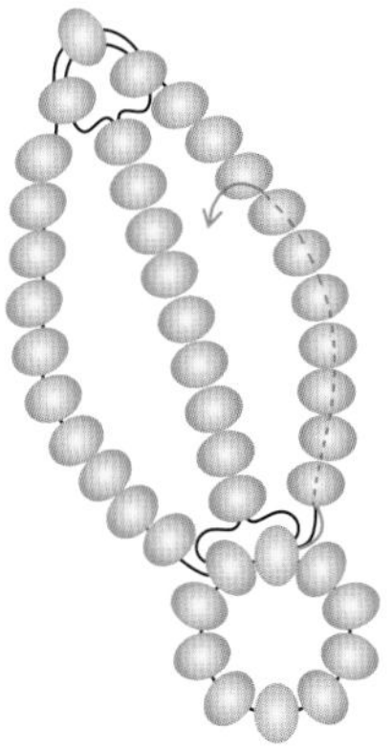

Thread on 1A and pass the needle down through the sixth A bead of the spike made in step 2 and the following 4A to emerge just above the first A bead of the spike (fig 6).

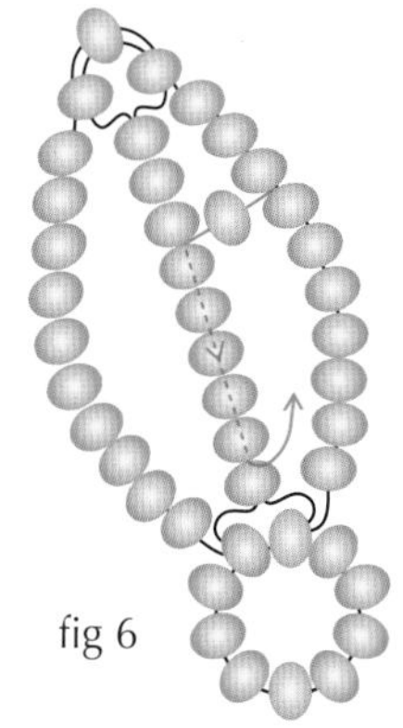

Thread on 3A. Pass the needle through the previous 3A on the central stem of the petal and the first 2A of the 3A just added (fig 7).

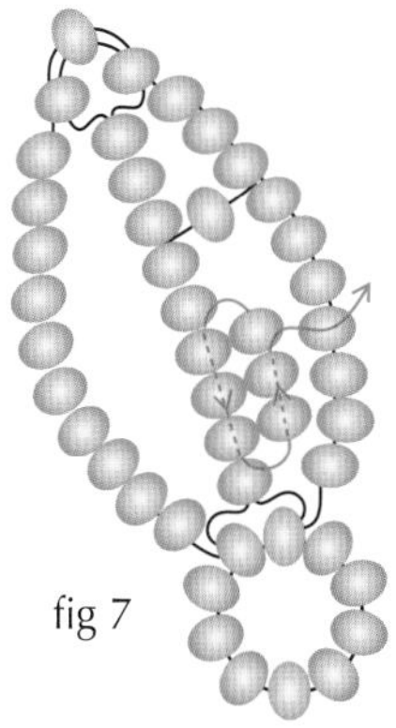

fig 5

fig 6

fig 7

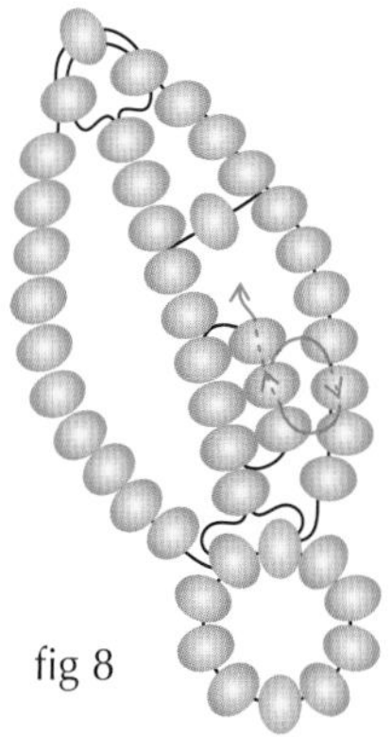

fig 8

5 Pass the needle down through the third A bead of the first side of the petal and back up the middle A bead of the 3A just added to bring the two beads parallel to one another.

Pass the needle through the following 1A (fig 8).

6 Pass the needle down through the 4A beads of the central petal stem and up the first 7A at the other side of the petal (fig 9).

Repeat steps 4 and 5 on this side of the central stem.

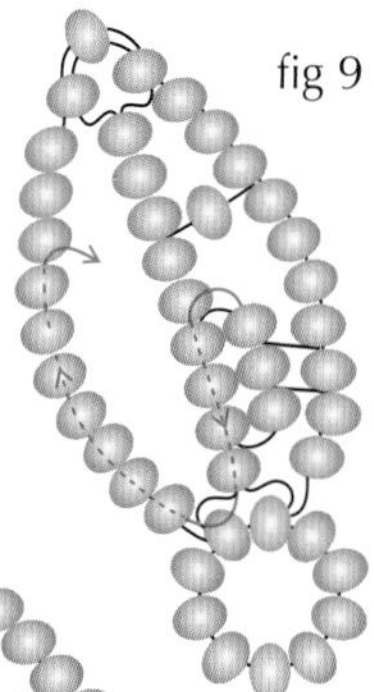

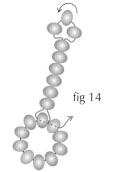

fig 9

7 Pass the needle down through the central petal stem, the 2A beads on the ring that support the petal and the following 2A beads of the ring to be in the correct place to start the next petal (fig 10).

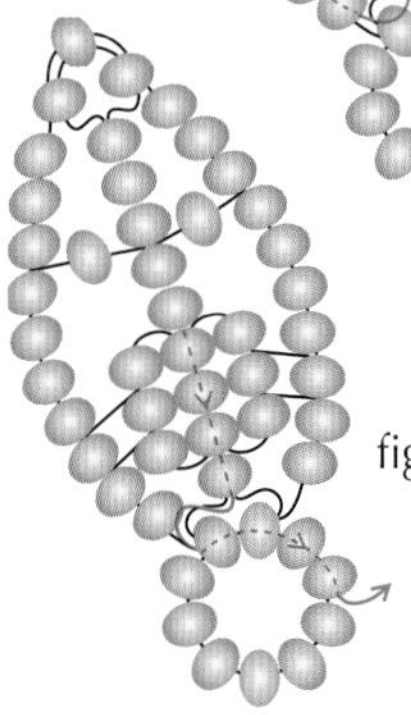

fig 10

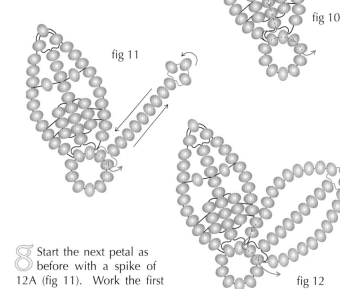

fig 11

8 Start the next petal as before with a spike of 12A (fig 11). Work the first side of the petal as in fig 3.

For the second side of the petal thread on 8A. Pass the needle down through the first 2A beads of the first side of the previous petal and the 2A beads of the ring (fig 12). Complete the remainder of the petal as before.

Repeat step 8 to make two more petals.

fig 12

9 The fifth petal needs to be joined to both petal one and petal four.

Start with a central spike of 12A as before.

Pass the needle up through the first 2A beads on the free side of the first petal (fig 13).

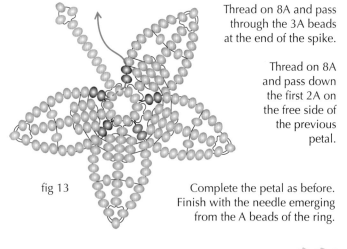

Thread on 8A and pass through the 3A beads at the end of the spike.

Thread on 8A and pass down the first 2A on the free side of the previous petal.

fig 13

Complete the petal as before. Finish with the needle emerging from the A beads of the ring.

10 The Trumpet - This is supported on the 10A beads of the central ring. For clarity the following diagrams do not show the flat petals already in situ.

Thread on 9A. Leaving aside the last 3A beads to form an anchor pass the needle back down the first 6A beads to make a spike of A beads.

Pass the needle through the single A bead on the ring at the base of the spike and the following 1A (fig 14).

fig 14

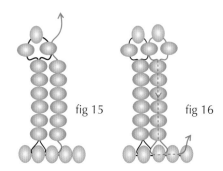

11 Thread on 6A. Pass the needle up through the first A bead of the anchor on the previous spike (fig 15) and thread on 2A.

fig 15   fig 16

Pass the needle down through the 6A beads, the single A bead at the base of the spike and the following 1A bead on the ring to bring the two spikes parallel to one another (fig 16).

Repeat step 11 seven more times to complete nine linked spikes.

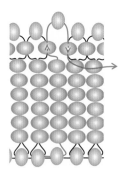

12 Thread on 6A. Pass the needle up through the first anchor bead of the previous spike and thread on 1A.

Pass the needle down through the last anchor bead of the first spike (fig 17).

Pass down the 6A beads just added and through the A bead on the ring at the base of the spike (as fig 16).

fig 17

13 Pass back up the beads of the last spike to emerge from the single A bead added at the very top of the spike (fig 18).

Thread on 1A and pass the needle through the A bead at the very top of the next spike around the top of the trumpet pulling the new bead into the gap between the two spike beads (fig 19).

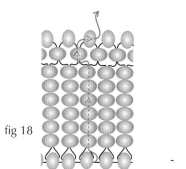

fig 18   -   fig 19

Repeat around the top rim of the trumpet to add nine more single A beads in total.

Pass the needle through the 20A beads that now make up the rim of the trumpet once more and back down through the beads of one of the spikes to emerge through an A bead on the ring.

Leave the thread ends attached and set aside for the moment.

14 The Leaves - Prepare the needle with 1.5m of single thread and tie a keeper bead 15cm from the end. The leaves are made in square stitch.

Thread on 4B for the first row.

Thread on 1B and pass the needle through the fourth B of the 4B in the same direction as before and back through the new B bead (fig 20) to turn the corner and make a square stitch.

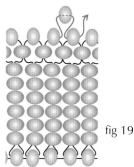

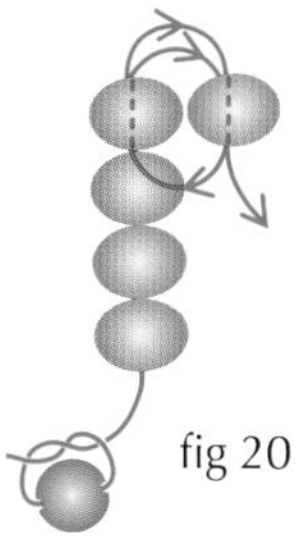

fig 20

Thread on 1B. Pass the needle through the third B of the 4B row and back through the new B bead (fig 21) to make a square stitch. Repeat to add a further two square stitches to the end of the row.

fig 21

Repeat to make six rows of 4B in total.

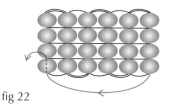

fig 22

15 The first and sixth rows now need to join together to make a drum.

Curl the rows into a cylinder four rows high.

Pass the needle up through the first B bead of the first row (shown flat in fig 22) and down through the last B bead of the sixth row to start the seam - link the other three beads on each row to their opposite number to make a little drum of beads four rows high and six beads around.

Finish with the needle emerging from the top edge of the drum.

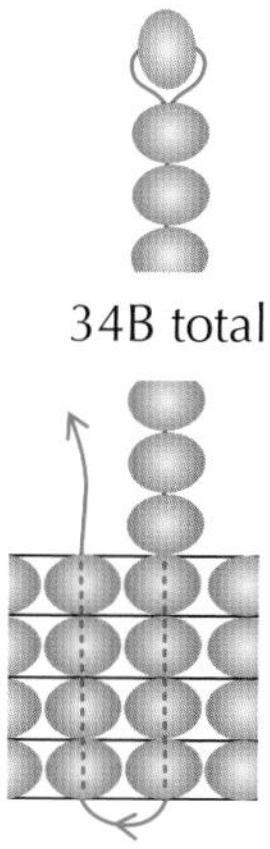

34B total

16 Thread on 34B.

Leaving aside the last B bead threaded to anchor the strand pass the needle back down the first 33B; the 4B of the drum below and up through the 4B of the next column of the drum (fig 23).

fig 23

fig 24

17 Thread on 1B and square stitch to the first B bead of the 34B stem (fig 24).

Continue to work up the stem to add 31B beads in total: finishing 3B beads short of the top of the 34B bead stem.

Pass the needle down the stem to emerge between the seventh and eighth B beads from the top of the stem (fig 25).

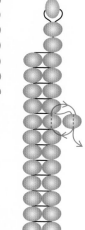

fig 25

fig 26

Thread on 1B and square stitch to the eighth B bead from the top of the stem (fig 26) - the needle should finish pointing down the stem towards the drum - see the Extra Info box below.

Square stitch 1B bead to each of the stem beads below this new B bead until you reach the drum at the base.

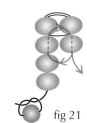

Extra Info....
If your needle is pointing in the wrong direction when compared to fig 26, you have stitched the new bead to the seventh bead from the top of the stem - not the eighth bead. Take the stitch out and try again.

Successfully managing the direction of the thread path is the key to success in many beadwork designs.

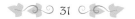

Dinky Daffodils

These tiny daffodils are quick and easy to make - they're perfect for making a necklace or using in a collage (see page 63).

You will need 0.8g of Delica beads or 0.5g of size 15/0 seed beads to make a Dinky Daffodil.

Make a circle of 10A as in step 1.

Referring to the technique in step 2, thread on 7A and make a spike with an anchor of 3A at the end (fig a).

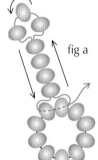

fig a

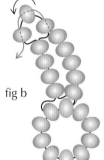

fig b

Following step 3 add 5A for each side of the first petal (fig b).

Referring to step 8 link the bottom of the second petal to the first petal by annexing the bottom A bead of the petal edge (fig c).

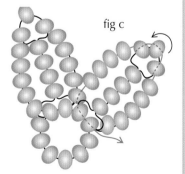

fig c

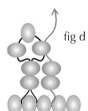

fig d

The trumpet is made with the same method as in steps 10 to 13 but it's much shorter. Thread on just 5A for the first spike in step 10 (fig d) and follow through the technique as before.

18 Pass the needle down through the 4B beads of the drum to emerge on the bottom edge.

Pass up through the first 2B beads of the next row along. Skip to one row further around the drum and pass up through the top 2B beads of that row to emerge at the top of the drum two beads along from the last square stitch row worked (fig 27).

This is the correct position to start the second leaf stem.

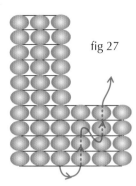

fig 27

19 Thread on 16B. As in fig 23 leave the last B bead threaded to anchor the top of the strand and pass the needle back down through the 15B below it; the 4B beads of the drum and up through the 4B beads of an adjacent drum row.

Starting with 1B (as fig 24) square stitch 12 single B beads up one side of the stem.

As in fig 25 pass the needle down through the beads of the central stem to emerge between the sixth and seventh B beads. Make the first square stitch going down to attach 1B to the seventh B bead from the top of the stem.

Work right down to the drum as before. Pass the needle through the 4B beads of the drum and finish off this thread end securely.

Leave the thread end at the bottom of the drum loose.

20 Assembling the Spray - Return to the thread end left at the back of the daffodil flower and reattach the needle. You need to attach the soldered jump ring to the back of the flower to allow the brooch pin to pass.

fig 28

Thread on 1D.

Pass the needle through the jump ring and back down the D bead.

Pull the jump ring up close to the D bead and the D bead up tight to the back of the flower.

Pass the needle through one of the 10A beads of the ring and back through the D bead to emerge alongside the jump ring (fig 28). Pass the needle through the jump ring again and back through the D bead to double up the thread holding the ring in place. Pass the needle through one of the 10A beads of the ring.

Leave the thread ends attached.

21 Thread 1C onto the headpin. Pass the headpin through the centre of the trumpet to emerge through the ring of 10A.

Carefully thread the end of the pin through the D bead added in step 20 to emerge just to one side of the jump ring (not through the ring).

Bend the headpin as close as you can behind the D bead to make an angle of 90° (fig 29).

Thread on sufficient B beads to reach within 8mm of the end of the headpin.

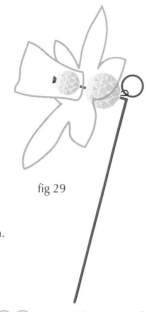

fig 29

fig 30

22 Thread the prepared leaf assembly onto the pin so that the bottom row of the drum lies flush with the bottom B bead just added to the pin (the B beads on the pin will fit snugly inside the drum).

Use the loose thread at the bottom of the drum to make a few stitches across the base to prevent the bottom D bead on the headpin from sneaking through. Finish off the thread end as before.

Carefully turn a loop at the end of the pin to use up all of the excess length and push all of the B beads up tight to one another.

Bend the loop where it meets the bottom B bead through 90° so that it sits parallel to the bottom of the leaf drum but sticks out slightly to the reverse of the spray (fig 32).

23 Twist the leaves around the flower until the longer of the two leaves makes a pleasing angle behind the daffodil petals and the shorter leaf comes just to the front of the flower.

Reattach the needle to one of the thread ends on the flower and slip-stitch the longer leaf into place creating one or two anchoring points between the flower and the leaf.

Finish off all the remaining thread ends neatly and securely.

fig 31

21 Completing the Pin - Thread 1D and a French crimp onto the pin and push up to the top. Crush the crimp with flat nosed pliers to keep the D bead in place.

Daffodil Pendant & Necklace

Using size 15/0 seed beads to make the daffodil flowers gives you very delicate 30mm blooms.

A 6mm jump ring slipped into a petal tip easily converts one of these flowers into an earring or a pendant for a fine chain.

Or link three flower heads together, one made with the standard pattern and two Dinky Daffodils, for a perfect bridesmaid's necklace.

To wear the pin - Thread the pin through the jump ring behind the flower, through the lapel of your garment and out though the loop at the end of the stem (fig 31). Push the pin guard over the point of the pin.

Eloise Necklace
& Bracelet

necklace measures 43cm
bracelet measures   20cm

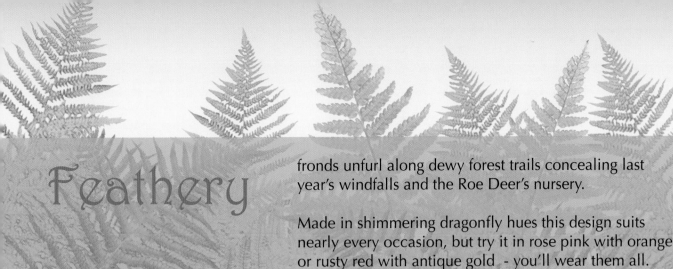

Feathery

fronds unfurl along dewy forest trails concealing last year's windfalls and the Roe Deer's nursery.

Made in shimmering dragonfly hues this design suits nearly every occasion, but try it in rose pink with orange or rusty red with antique gold - you'll wear them all.

You Will Need

To Make the Necklace

10g of size 10/0 opaque blue scarab seed beads A
1.5g of DB1206 silver lined lime Delica beads B
1.5g of DB1208 silver lined teal Delica beads C
1g of DB0285 lined blue aqua Delica beads D
Six 6mm tanzanite fire polished faceted beads E
Eight 6mm turquoise fire polished faceted beads F
Four 4mm tanzanite fire polished faceted beads G
Black size D beading thread

To Make the Bracelet

A, B, C and D in same quantities as for the necklace
Nine 4mm tanzanite fire polished faceted beads H
Nine 4mm turquoise fire polished faceted beads J
One 6mm turquoise fire polished faceted bead K
One 6mm tanzanite fire polished faceted bead L

Tools

A size 10 beading needle
A pair of scissors to trim the threads

The Necklace is Made in Three Stages

The basic framework for the front of the necklace is made first.
The framework sections are then embellished with graduated strands and faceted glass beads.
The side straps are added to the desired length.

1 The Framework - Prepare the needle with 1.5m of single thread and tie a keeper bead 15cm from the end.

fig 1

Thread on 4A. Pass the needle through the first 2A of the 4A to bring the beads into two columns of 2A beads (fig 1).

fig 2

2 Thread on 14A.
Pass the needle through the first 2A of the 4A and the following 3A of the new beads to produce a ring of 16A beads with the needle emerging from the 3rd bead of the lower edge (fig 2).

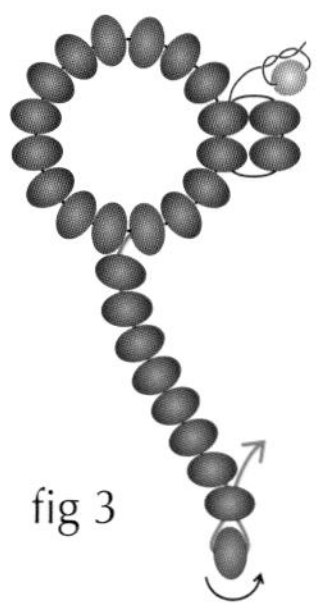

3 Thread on 9A. Leaving aside the last A bead to anchor the strand, pass the needle back up the eighth A bead just added (fig 3).

Thread on 10A and pass the needle up through the second column of 2A made in step 1 to make a link (fig 4).

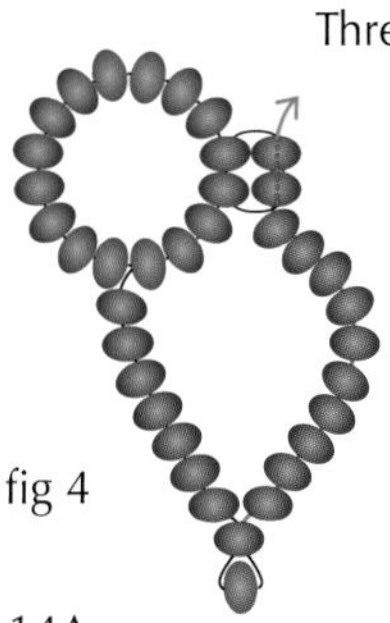

fig 3

fig 4

4 Thread on 14A.

Referring to fig 5 pass the needle up through the fifth and fourth A beads below the last link. Pass back down the last two A beads of the 14A just added to make a new link (fig 5).

fig 5

5 Thread on 10A. Following fig 6 leave the last 1A aside to anchor the strand and pass the needle back up through the ninth A bead.

Thread on 15A.

Locate the fourth and fifth A beads above the last link (made in fig 5). Pass the needle down through these two beads and up the last 2A of the 15A just added (fig 6).

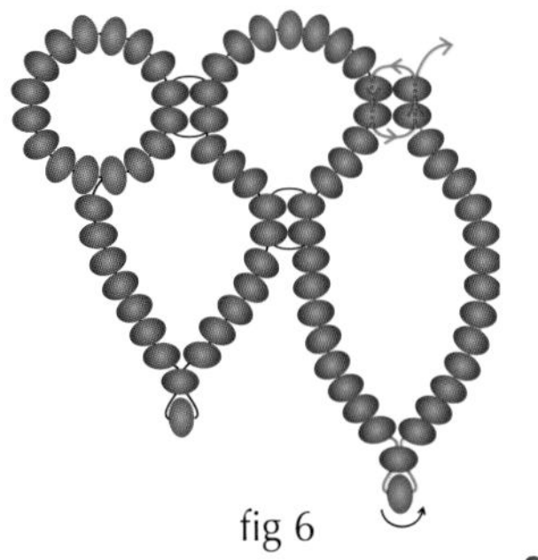

fig 6

6 Thread on 14A and following fig 7 make a link to the fourth and fifth A beads below the last link.

fig 7

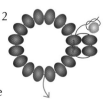

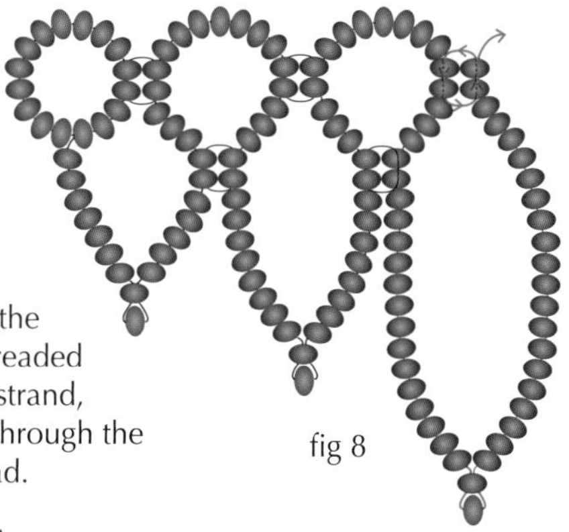

7 Thread on 16A.

Leaving aside the last A bead threaded to anchor the strand, pass back up through the fifteenth A bead.

Thread on 21A. Link the last two A beads threaded to the fourth and fifth A beads above the last link (fig 8).

fig 8

8 Repeat from step 4 to step 7 twice.

Repeat from step 4 to the end of step 6 once.

Thread on 9A. Make the anchor at the bottom as before and thread on 12A. Make a link to the fourth and fifth A beads above the last link to complete a smaller, pointed motif to match the other end of the work.

fig 9

9 Thread on 11A.

Pass the needle up through the 3A beads below the last link and the following 2A beads of the link. Pass down through the adjacent 2A of the link (fig 9).

The work should now be symmetrical.

fig 10

10 Embellishing the Motifs - Thread on 5A and 1B.

Following fig 10 pass the needle down through the three beads above the anchor at the base of the frame and through the anchor bead.

Pass back up the other side of the frame to emerge three beads above the anchor on that side of the frame (fig 10).

fig 11

11 Thread on 1B. Pass the needle up through the bottom 2A beads of the central 5A stem (see fig 11).

Thread on 2C. Count 2A beads up the edge of the frame from the first B bead and pass the needle through this bead (fig 11).

12 Pass the needle back through the 2C beads just added and through 1A bead of the 5A stem to emerge on the other side of the central 5A stem (fig 12).

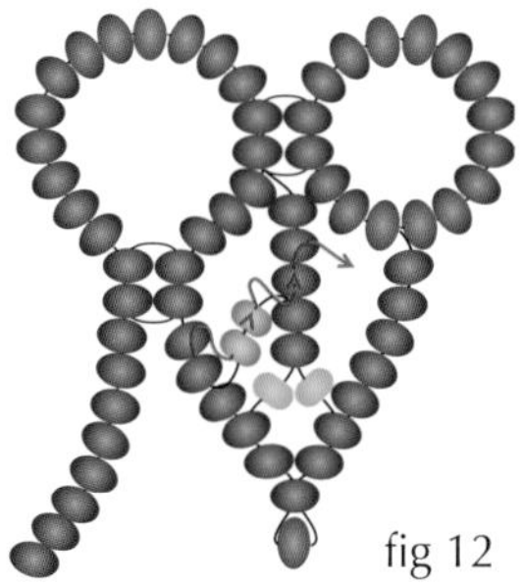

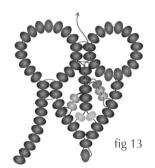

fig 12

fig 13

Thread on 1D and 2C. Count 2A beads up from the previous B bead stitch on this side of the frame. Pass the needle through this A bead, back up through the C and D beads and the top two A beads of the central stem.

Pass up through the 2A beads of the link closest to the end of the design (fig 13).

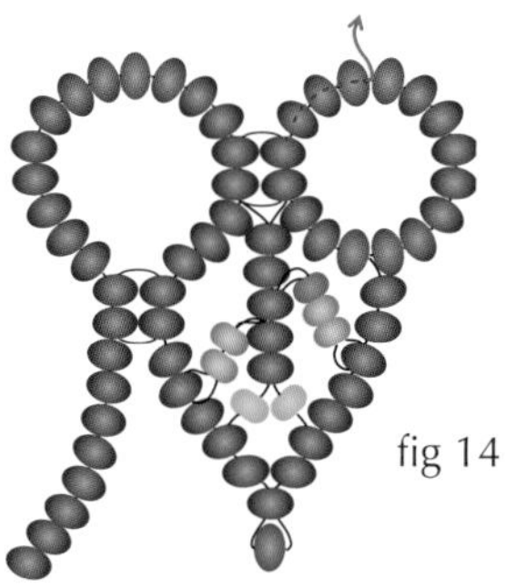

Pass through the following 3A beads of the end ring (fig 14).

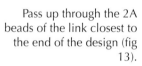

fig 14

13 Thread on 1F and pass through the eighth A bead around the ring.

Pass back through the F bead and the A bead at the far end in the same direction (fig 15).

Pass through the F bead again and the eighth A bead of the ring to finish with the needle pointing towards the end of the beadwork (fig 16).

fig 15

fig 16

Referring to fig 17 pass through the following A beads around the ring and the closest 2A beads of the link.

Turn and pass up through the adjacent 2A beads of the link and the following 4A of the next ring.

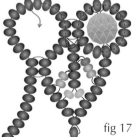

fig 17

14 Referring to fig 18 thread on 1E.

Pass down through 2A of the link below the ring and up the adjacent 2A of the link.

Pass back up the E bead and the A bead at the top of the ring in the same direction.

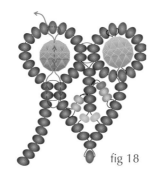

fig 18

15 Referring to fig 19 pass through the following 3A of the ring and 2A beads of the link.

Thread on 8A for the stem down the centre of the next frame.

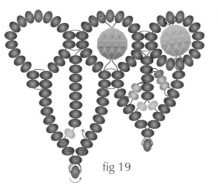

fig 19

16 Thread on 1B. Pass the needle through the 3A beads above the anchor bead, the anchor bead and the three beads above the anchor on the other side of the frame (fig 19).

Thread on 1B and pass the needle up the bottom 2A beads of the 8A stem (fig 20).

fig 20

17 Fig 21 shows the next five ribs alternating from one side of the frame to the other.

Referring to fig 21 throughout, thread on 1C and 1B. Count 2A up the opposite edge of the frame and pass the needle through this bead. Pass back up the B and C beads and 1A bead of the central stem to emerge on the opposite side of the stem.

Thread on 1C and 1B. Count 2A up this edge of the frame and pass the needle through this bead. Pass back up the B and C beads and 1A of the stem.

Maintaining the alternating pattern as shown in fig 21 thread on 2C and 1B. Count 2A up the edge of the frame and pass the needle through this bead. Pass the needle back up the B and C beads and 1A of the stem.

Make the next rib with 1D, 1C and 1B passing up through 1A on the stem to be in the correct position for the last rib.

Make the final rib with 2D and 2C (fig 21).

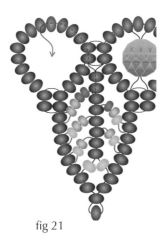

fig 21

18 Pass up through the 2A beads of the link above and the following 4A beads of the ring (fig 21).

Add an F bead to the centre of this ring as you added the E bead in fig 18. Pass down through the remaining beads of the ring and the first 2A beads of the next link to be in the correct position to add the central stem and ribs to the next frame along.

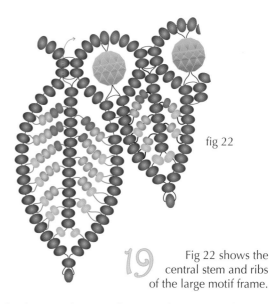

fig 22

19 Fig 22 shows the central stem and ribs of the large motif frame.

Make the central stem with 14A and 1B passing through the beads of the anchor as before.

Add the second single B bead and pass back up the bottom 2A beads of the new stem ready to add the next rib.

Spacing the ribs as before add the following -

2B - first rib on the left
2B - first rib on the right
2C and 1B - second rib on the left
2C and 1B - second rib on the right
3C and 1B - third rib on the left
3C and 1B - third rib on the right
1D, 3C and 1B - fourth rib on the left
1D, 3C and 1B - fourth rib on the right
2D and 3C - fifth rib on the left
2D and 2C - fifth rib on the right
2D and 2C - sixth rib on the left

Pass to the top of the stem.

As in fig 21 pass up through the 2A beads of the link and the following 4A beads of the ring. Add an E bead to the centre of the ring as in fig 18.

20 Repeat step 15 to step 19 twice more.

Repeat step 15 to step 18 once only.

Repeat step 10 to step 12 to add the stem and ribs to the last frame. Add the E bead to the last circle as in fig 15.

Finish off the all the remaining thread ends neatly and securely without blocking the holes in the frame beads at either end of the work.

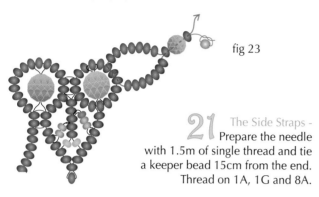

fig 23

21 The Side Straps - Prepare the needle with 1.5m of single thread and tie a keeper bead 15cm from the end. Thread on 1A, 1G and 8A.

Referring to fig 23 pass through the middle 3A free beads at the edge of the end ring of the centrepiece.

Thread on 7A and pass the needle through the first A bead of the 8A, the G bead and the following 1A to emerge alongside the keeper bead (fig 23).

22 Thread on 1C, 1B, 1A, 1F, 1A, 1B, 1C, 1A, 1G, 1C, 1B and 1C. Thread on sufficient A beads to make this side of the design up to the desired length - make a note of this number.

23 The Bead Tag - Thread on 1C, 1B, 1F, 1B, 1C, 1B, 1E, 1B, 1C and 3A. Leaving aside the last 3A beads to anchor the strand pass back through the last C bead and the following beads just added to emerge just after the first C bead (fig 24).

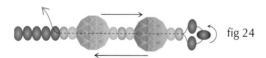

fig 24

24 Thread on the same number of A beads as noted in step 22 to make the second strand of the strap.

Referring to fig 25 pass through the last C bead added in step 22 and the following beads to emerge through the middle A bead of the 3A on the edge of the ring.

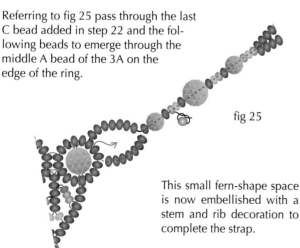

fig 25

This small fern-shape space is now embellished with a stem and rib decoration to complete the strap.

25 Thread on 3A and 1B. Referring to fig 26 pass the needle through an A bead two beads up from the tip of the motif.

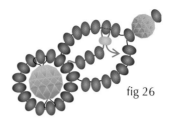

fig 26

Pass back through the B bead (fig 26).

Thread on 1B. Pass the needle through the corresponding A bead on the other side of the frame and back through the new B bead.

fig 27

Pass the needle through the end 2A beads of the stem (fig 27).

26 Referring to fig 28 thread on 1C and 1B. Pass the needle through the second A bead along the edge of the frame and back through the B and C beads.

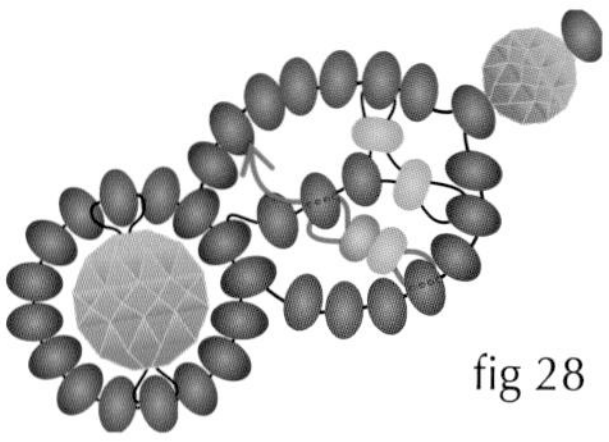

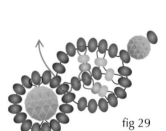

fig 28

Pass through the second A bead from the end of the stem once more in the same direction as before to draw the new rib up close to the A bead - the needle will be pointing towards the centre front of the design (fig 28).

Make a similar rib on the other side of the fern motif (see fig 29).

fig 29

Pass back to the start of the stem and through the middle A bead of the 3A of the ring (fig 29).

Finish off the thread ends neatly and securely.

27 Repeat steps 21 and 22 on the other side of the centrepiece. You now need to add the bead loop part of the clasp.

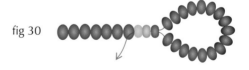

fig 30

The Bead Loop - Thread on 1B, 1C and 1B followed by sufficient A beads to make a loop that will just fit over the E and F beads of the bead tag (approximately 17A). Pass back down the B, C and B beads to draw up the loop (fig 30).

Repeat steps 24 to 26 to complete the strap and the final motif. Finish off all the remaining thread ends neatly and securely.

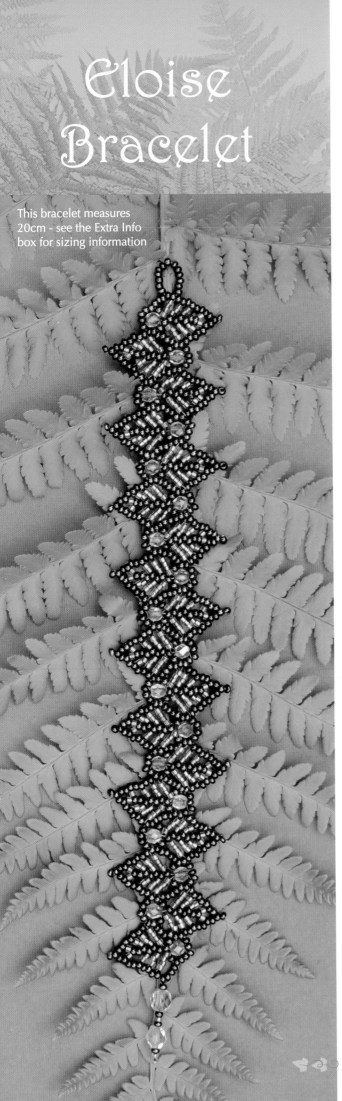

Eloise Bracelet

This bracelet measures 20cm - see the Extra Info box for sizing information

The Bracelet is Made in Two Stages

The basic framework for the fern motifs is made first. The framework sections are then embellished with graduated strands and faceted glass beads.

Extra Info....

Each fern motif will add 11mm to the length of the bracelet and the clasp will add up to 20mm of extra length. With this information to hand calculate how many fern motifs you need to make.

28 The Framework - Prepare the needle with 1.5m of single thread and tie a keeper bead 15cm from the end. Thread on 1H and 4A.

Pass the needle through the H bead a second time to bring the 4A into a strap on one side of the H bead (fig 31).

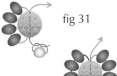

fig 31

fig 32

Thread on 4A and pass through the H bead again to make a second strap on the other side (fig 32).

Pass the needle through the first 3A beads of the second strap (fig 33).

fig 33

29 Thread on 15A. Leaving aside the last A bead to make an anchor pass back up the fourteenth A bead just added (fig 34).

fig 34

Thread on 13A. Pass up through the second, third and fourth A beads on the first strap of 4A (fig 35).

fig 35

fig 36

30 Thread on 2A. Pass through the first 3A beads of the second strap and the following 6A beads along the edge of the motif (fig 36). This will draw the 2A beads into the gap above the hole in the H bead.

fig 37

31 Thread on 1A, 1J and 1A. Pass through the last two A beads threaded through in fig 36. Pass through the first A bead just added and the following 1J (fig 37). This effectively creates a strap of 4A on one side of the new J bead.

32 Thread on 4A and pass the needle back up the J bead again to make a strap of 4A on the other side (fig 38).

Pass the needle through the 4A beads on the first strap around the J bead. Thread on 2A and pass the needle through the first 3A beads of the second strap (fig 39).

fig 38

fig 39

fig 40

fig 41

33 Thread on 15A. As before leave aside the last A bead threaded to anchor the strand and pass the needle back through the previous bead to make the point of the new motif (fig 40).

Thread on 7A. Following fig 41 pass the needle through the middle 2A beads of the strap of 4A around the previous faceted bead, the following 4A beads leading up to the strap around the next faceted bead, 8A around the edge of this faceted bead and 6A along the following edge (fig 41).

Notice that there are 2A beads on the inner edge of the faceted beads that are not passed through.

You are now in the correct place to start the next motif.

Repeat step 31 noticing that the needle is pointing in the opposite direction - see fig 42. Repeat steps 32 and 33 to complete a motif pointing in the opposite direction (fig 43).

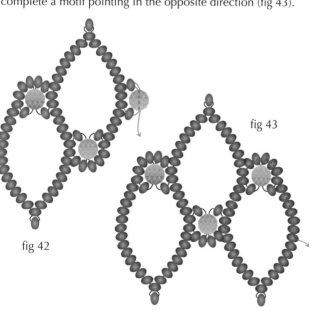

fig 42

fig 43

34 Repeat steps 31 to 33 using J beads instead of H beads. Revert to H for the next two motifs.

Repeat this sequence of two J motifs and two H motifs until the band is the required number of motifs long - see Extra Info on page 39.

Complete the last motif up to fig 41 with the needle emerging from the sixth A bead along the edge.

35 The Clasp Loop - Thread on 16A. Pass the needle through the previous 2A on the edge of the motif (fig 44). Check that the K and L beads for the bead tag will just fit through the loop created. If necessary adjust the bead count. Reinforce the bead loop by passing the needle through these A beads once more.

fig 44

fig 45

Referring to fig 45 pass through the A beads around the edge of the motif to emerge from the faceted bead into the central space of the motif. This is the correct position to begin the embellishment.

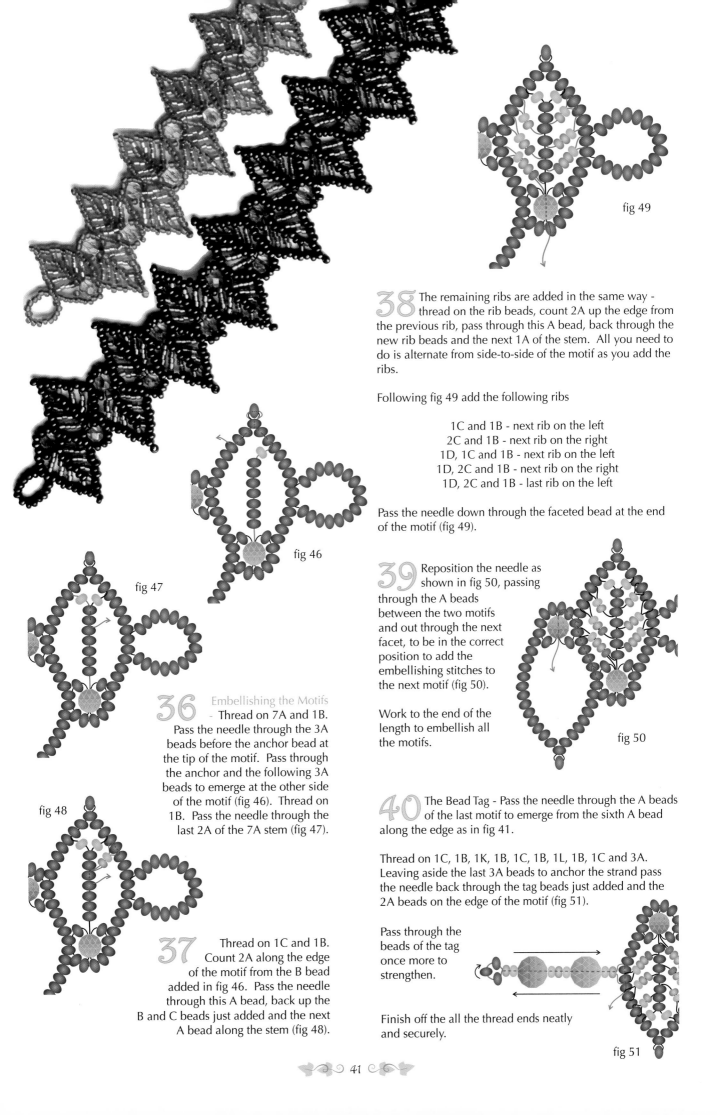

fig 49

38 The remaining ribs are added in the same way - thread on the rib beads, count 2A up the edge from the previous rib, pass through this A bead, back through the new rib beads and the next 1A of the stem. All you need to do is alternate from side-to-side of the motif as you add the ribs.

Following fig 49 add the following ribs

1C and 1B - next rib on the left
2C and 1B - next rib on the right
1D, 1C and 1B - next rib on the left
1D, 2C and 1B - next rib on the right
1D, 2C and 1B - last rib on the left

Pass the needle down through the faceted bead at the end of the motif (fig 49).

39 Reposition the needle as shown in fig 50, passing through the A beads between the two motifs and out through the next facet, to be in the correct position to add the embellishing stitches to the next motif (fig 50).

Work to the end of the length to embellish all the motifs.

fig 50

fig 46

fig 47

36 Embellishing the Motifs - Thread on 7A and 1B. Pass the needle through the 3A beads before the anchor bead at the tip of the motif. Pass through the anchor and the following 3A beads to emerge at the other side of the motif (fig 46). Thread on 1B. Pass the needle through the last 2A of the 7A stem (fig 47).

fig 48

37 Thread on 1C and 1B. Count 2A along the edge of the motif from the B bead added in fig 46. Pass the needle through this A bead, back up the B and C beads just added and the next A bead along the stem (fig 48).

40 The Bead Tag - Pass the needle through the A beads of the last motif to emerge from the sixth A bead along the edge as in fig 41.

Thread on 1C, 1B, 1K, 1B, 1C, 1B, 1L, 1B, 1C and 3A. Leaving aside the last 3A beads to anchor the strand pass the needle back through the tag beads just added and the 2A beads on the edge of the motif (fig 51).

Pass through the beads of the tag once more to strengthen.

Finish off the all the thread ends neatly and securely.

fig 51

Kyoto
Necklace

necklace measures 42cm

Boulevards

where the softest velvet pink and translucent pearl white petals touch branch tips over the heads of entranced hanami strollers throughout Japan. Hanami means flower-viewing and is a national pastime throughout the cherry blossom or Sakura season.

You Will Need

To Make the Necklace

5g of size 15/0 white lined crystal AB seed beads A
1g of size 15/0 pale yellow lined crystal AB seed beads B
7g of size 15/0 opaque olive AB seed beads C
9g of size 15/0 golden olive lustre seed beads D
1g of size 8/0 dark bronze metallic seed beads E
Ten 4mm gold sparkle metallic beads F
Seven 6mm pearl beads G
Three 4mm pearl beads H
30cm of 0.8mm half-hard silver plated wire
Ash size D beading thread
White size D beading thread

Tools

A size 13 beading needle
A pair of scissors to trim the threads
A pair of wire cutters

Extra Info....

Making successful blossom flowers is all about controlling the tension in the thread. Don't pull the brick stitch too tight in steps 2 and 3 or you will pucker the ring. However when you reach steps 6 and 7 you will need to pull the thread a little more to make the petals curl and to make the stamens stand upright.

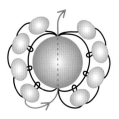

The Necklace is Made in Five Stages

The three open blossoms are made using brick stitch.
The four larger buds are made next.
The herringbone rope branch for the front of the design is made and threaded with a wire core.
The large buds and open blossoms are attached and the ends of the branches tapered by the addition of small buds.
The side straps are added to complete the necklace.

1 The Open Blossoms - Prepare the needle with 1.5m of single white thread and tie a keeper bead 15cm from the end. Thread on 1F.

fig 1   Pass the needle through the F bead again to make a strap of thread on the side (fig 1). Repeat (fig 2).   fig 2

2 Thread on 2A.
Pass the needle under the first thread strap adjacent to the F bead hole and back up the second A bead (fig 3) - the 2A should sit side-by-side with the holes parallel.

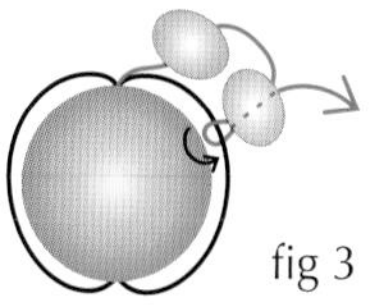

fig 3

Thread on 1A. Pass the needle under the thread strap and back up the new A to bring it alongside the previous A (fig 4).

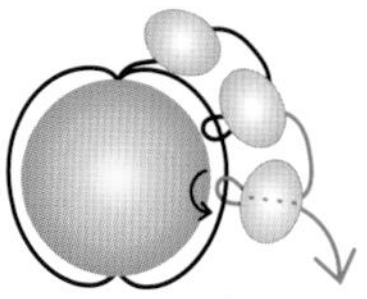

fig 4

This is brick stitch.

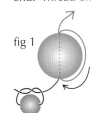

fig 5

Thread on 1A and make one more brick stitch. Pass the needle through the F bead (fig 5).

Repeat step 2 along the second thread strap (fig 6).

fig 6

3 Pass up through the first A bead and thread on 1A.
Pass up the first A bead again and down through the new A to bring the beads parallel (fig 7).

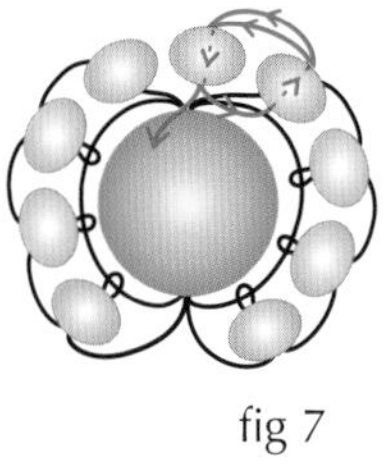

Pass up the first A bead on the other strap and down through the new A and the F bead (fig 8).

fig 7

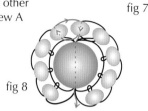

fig 8

You have added 1A to bridge the gap above the F bead hole.

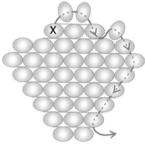

fig 9

Repeat at the current needle position to complete a ring of 10A around the F bead (fig 9).

4 Fig 11 shows the grid for the petals. Each petal is supported by 2A beads on the ring. To start the petal you need to add the two beads at the bottom of the grid.

Pass the needle through the closest A bead and thread on 2A.

Pass the needle down the adjacent A bead of the ring, back up the previous A and the first A just added (fig 10).

This completes the first row of the grid.

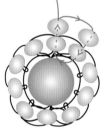

fig 10

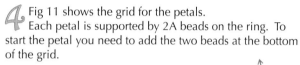
X
fig 11

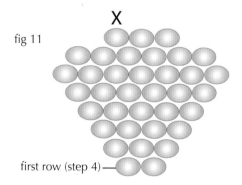

first row (step 4) —

5 Add the 3A beads of the second row in brick stitch starting with a 2A stitch (fig 12).

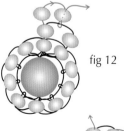

fig 12

Thread on 1A for the last bead of the row and referring to fig 13 pass down the A at the end of the previous row and up the 2A at the other edge of the petal ready to start the next row.

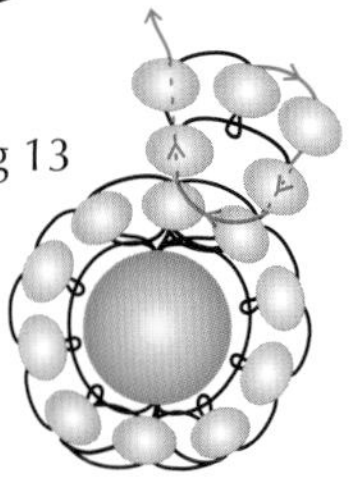

fig 13

Work the remainder of the grid in A beads using standard brick stitch.

6 The needle should be emerging from the bead marked X on fig 11.

Referring to fig 14 thread on 2A and pass down the first A of the last row worked. Thread on 1A and pass through the edge bead of the next row down and the following five edge beads pulling the thread quite firmly to start to curl the petal (fig 14).

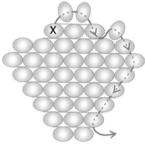

fig 14

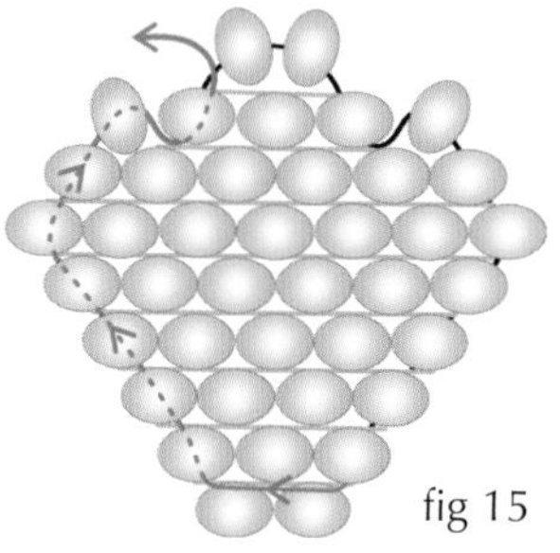

Referring to fig 15 pass the needle across the front of the petal and up the 6A on the other edge.

Thread on 1A and pass up through the last A bead added (bead X). Again pull the thread quite firmly - the petal should form a shallow cup.

fig 15

Pass the needle down through the beads of the other edge to the A bead ring and up through the next 1A ready to make the next petal (fig 16).

Repeat from step 4 to step 6 to complete the remaining four petals - make sure they all curve to the front of the flower motif.

Finish with the needle against the F bead at the base of the last petal.

fig 16

7 The stamens sit on the junction between the A beads of the ring and the F bead at the centre of the flower. The stitches attach to the thread loops around the F bead.

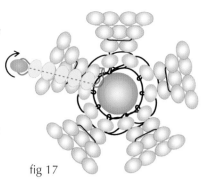

If necessary pass the needle through to the front of the flower adjacent to the F bead. Thread on 5B and 1C.

fig 17

Leaving aside the C bead to anchor the strand, pass the needle down through the 5B beads and through the gap between the last A bead passed through and the next A bead around the ring (fig 17). Pull the thread firmly to make the stamen stand straight.

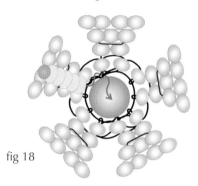

fig 18

Pass the needle to the front of the flower through the gap between the F bead and the thread loop (fig 18).

Thread on 4B and 1C. As before leave aside the C bead for the anchor and pass back down the 4B.

Pass the needle to the back of the flower through the next gap between the A beads of the ring and the innermost thread strap (as fig 17) - this keeps the stamen close to the F bead.

Repeat to make ten stamens in total alternating 4B and 1C, and 5B and 1C, to frame the F bead.

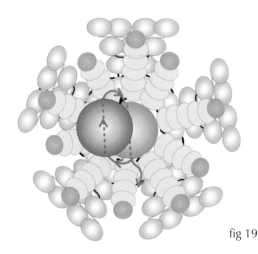

fig 19

8 Pass the needle through the F bead to emerge at the front of the flower inside the stamen frame.

Thread on 1F. Pass to the back of the flower and through the first F to sit the new F on top of the first F and in the centre of the stamens (fig 19).

Remove the needle and set aside without finishing off the thread ends.

Repeat to make two more flowers to match.

9 The Large Buds - Each bud wraps five A bead petals around a G bead core.

Prepare the needle with 1m of single white thread and tie a keeper bead 15cm from the end. Thread on 1G.

10 Thread on 8A. Pass the needle through the G bead to bring the 8A into a strap on the side (fig 20).

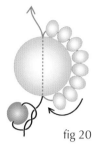

Pass the needle through the first 1A of the strap, thread on 5A and pass the needle through the last 2A of the strap (fig 21).

fig 20

Pass the needle through the G bead.

11 Pass the needle down the first 4A of the first strap and thread on 1A.

Pass the needle up through the corresponding 4A of the second strap placing the new A bead between the straps with the needle emerging at the top of the strap (fig 22).

fig 21

Thread on 1A and pass down the 8A of the first strap to pull the new A into a tip for the petal (fig 23).

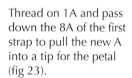

fig 22

fig 23

Pass the needle through the G bead.

Repeat steps 10 and 11 four more times to complete five petals.

fig 24

12 The needle should be emerging from the G bead between the petal tips. Thread on 1B and pass back through the G bead to position the new bead between the tips (fig 24).

To refine the details of the bud a calyx strand is now added between each petal pairing. Thread on 4C.

13 Referring to fig 25 pass the needle down through the fourth A bead along the side of the first petal edge and back up through the last C to make a square stitch.

Square stitch this 1C to the corresponding A bead on the adjacent petal (fig 26).

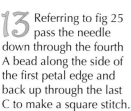

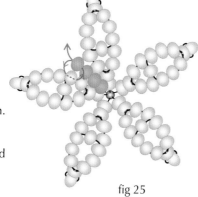

fig 25

fig 26

fig 27

Pass the needle through the same A bead on the first petal again and pass through the 3C below the square stitch (fig 27).

14 Thread on 5C.

Repeat step 13 to add a calyx strand between the second and third petals.

When the calyx strand is complete the needle should emerge 3C below the two square stitches just made (fig 28). The first 1C of the 5C is left to form a bridge between this calyx strand and the previous strand.

Repeat step 14 three more times.

fig 28

15 Thread on 1C and pass up through the 4C of the first calyx strand to make a bridge between the last and first strands. As in fig 27 pass the needle through the adjacent A bead of the petal and down through the first 3C below the square stitch.

Pass the needle through the 5C beads of the bridges between the calyx strands to bring them into a neat circle (fig 29).

Leave the thread end loose and remove the needle.

Repeat steps 9 to 15 to make one large bud to match.

Repeat step 9 to fig 24 in step 12 twice to make two buds without calyx strands.

fig 29

16 The Herringbone Rope Branch -
If required 'Herringbone Rope for Beginners' can be found on page 11.

Prepare the needle with 2m of single ash-coloured thread and tie a keeper bead 50cm from the end.

Thread on 3C and 1D. Pass the needle through the first C bead to make a ring (fig 30).

fig 30

Using this ring as the base for a four-bead herringbone stitch rope, work sufficient rows of 2C, and 1C and 1D, to make a 3cm length. Read the Extra Info box below and test out the wire.

> ### Extra Info....
> You will need to thread the 0.8mm wire down the centre of this herringbone rope. If you work with a tight tension the central space along the full 22.5cm length of rope might be too narrow to allow the wire to pass. Test the wire for fit when you have 3cm of rope - if it's very tight you will need to work the rope with the wire *in situ* - it will save a struggle later on.

If you are working your herringbone rope around the wire make sure that you have at least 12mm of wire showing at the start. You will also find it easier if you straighten the wire first - it will catch less often on your thread.

Continue with the four-bead herringbone stitch rope of 2C, and 1C and 1D, to complete a 22.5cm un-stretched length. The D beads should make a continuous single line along one corner of the rope. Leave the thread end loose.

17 If you have worked the rope away from the wire, now is the time to carefully thread the 0.8mm wire down the centre of the herringbone rope. It needs to stick out equally at either end.

Tie a short length of spare thread around the herringbone rope 12.5cm from one end - this temporary marker indicates position X on fig 31.

The first bend is at position X - you will need to make a drop-shaped loop. Referring to fig 31, which is drawn to scale, use a 10-11mm cylindrical mould (such as the barrel of a pen) to bend the wired rope at the thread marker. The wired rope needs to cross over, at position Y, 20-24mm from the marker. Make sure the longer rope end crosses to the front of the shorter rope end so you are starting the twist with the correct rotation.

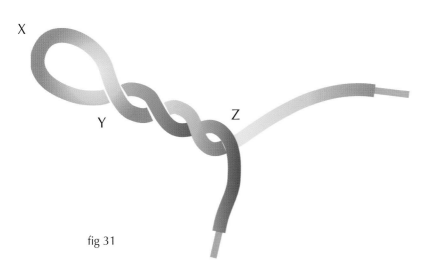

X

Y   Z

fig 31

Twist the two sides of the wired rope together twice (35mm of twist) and separate the ends (position Z).

The shorter rope end should measure 22-25mm and will become the vertical branch at the centre front. This rope end should finish at the front of the twist.

The longer rope end should measure 40-44mm and sweep out to form the plain branch to the right of the centrepiece.

If your rope has turned out to be a little short of these measurements add a few rows of herringbone stitch to the end and ease the work along the wire.

Trim the two wire ends 8mm from the ends of the rope.

18 Attaching the Buds - Push a large bud (without calyx straps) onto the wire end at the centre front - the wire should thread into the G bead hole but not emerge at the far end of the G bead alongside the B bead. Repeat at the other end of the wire with the matching bud.

The ends of the herringbone rope need to stretch a little to cover the gap between the rope and the back of the buds - this small amount of tension will keep the buds snugly in place. If the gap is larger than 3mm the wire will be forced through the end of the bud. If this is the case remove the bud and trim the wire a little.

19 Reattach the needle to the end of the rope. Thread on 4C. Stitch the last C bead to the fourth A beads of the adjacent two petals as in step 13.

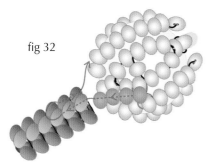

fig 32

Pass the needle down into the top two beads of the rope and out through the adjacent 2C ready to make the next calyx strap (fig 32).

Repeat to add calyx straps, from the remaining three beads at the end of the herringbone rope, into the next three petal gaps.

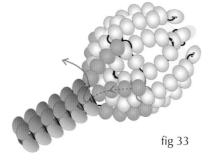

The fifth strap will have to be made from the gap between the first and last straps (fig 33).

fig 33

Leave the thread end attached and remove the needle.

Remove the keeper bead at the other end of the rope. Repeat step 19 to make the caylx straps to attach the bud at this end of the rope.

20 The Small Buds - Make sure the needle is attached to the thread end at the centre front and is pointing downwards from the end of the rope.

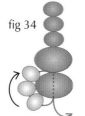

fig 34

Thread on 23C and 2E. Thread on 3A and pass through the second E bead again to make a strap of 3A on the side (fig 34).

Repeat this stitch six times to make seven straps in total.

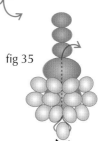

fig 35

Thread on 1A and pass the needle back up through the E bead and the following 1E (fig 35).

Pass the needle through the 23C of the string and the following two beads at the end of the rope.

21 Turn and (as fig 32) pass back down the adjacent column of the rope and through the first 8C of the string.

Thread on 6C, 1E and 1H.

Thread on 5A and pass the needle through the H bead to make a strap on the side (fig 36).
As before, repeat the stitch to add six further straps of 5A.

Thread on 1A and pass back up though the H bead (as fig 35) and the following 1E and 14C to emerge at the end of the herringbone rope.

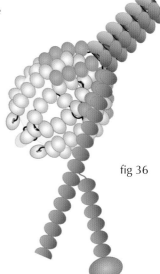

fig 36

22 Turn through the beads at the end of the rope and pass down through the top 3C of the string. Thread on 6C, 1E and 1H. Repeat as for the previous H bead making seven straps of 5A and returning the needle to the end of the herringbone rope.

Pass the needle up through 5-8 beads of the rope and finish off the thread end neatly and securely.

23 Attach the needle to the thread at the other end of the branch. Weave back along the top edge of the rope to emerge 4 rows from the end of the herringbone rope. Thread on 25C and 2E.

Convert the last E bead into a small bud as in step 20 by adding seven straps of 3A. Add the single A bead as in fig 35 and pass the needle back to the herringbone rope.

Turn the needle through the beads of the rope and pass back through the first 14C of the strand. Thread on 6C, 1E and 1H. As before, convert the H bead into a bud with seven straps of 5A. Add 1A (as fig 35) and pass the needle back to the herring-bone rope through the beads of the strand. Leave the thread attached and remove the needle.

24 Thread 1E onto the thread at the back of each of the remaining two large buds.

Offer these buds up to the branch just below the right-hand large bud - they need to nestle quite close together at the front of the branch (see photographs on pages 48 and 50). Use the thread ends from the buds to stitch them in place onto the rope. Trail the E bead below the last bud into the body of the rope with 3 or 4C beads to imitate a small stalk.

25 Offer the open blossoms up to the branch. Place one halfway down the central vertical branch and two, side-by-side, over the twisted branch section.
Adjust until the arrangement pleases.

Stitch into place using the thread ends remaining at the backs of the blossoms.

Leaving the loose thread end behind the large bud cluster to the right, finish off all other thread ends neatly and securely.

26 The Straps - Prepare the needle with 2.2m of single ash-coloured thread and tie a keeper bead 70cm from the end.
Thread on 3D and 1C. Pass the needle through the first D bead to make a ring (as fig 30). Using this ring, as the base for a four-bead herringbone rope, work sufficient rows of 2D, and 1C and 1D, to make 11cm of length with the C beads making a continuous single line along one corner of the rope.

Leave the thread end loose - you will return to set the final length and add the clasp in step 30.

27 Remove the keeper bead at the start of the rope and attach the needle to this thread end.

Thread on 1E, 1G, 1E, 1F and 2D. Pass the needle back through the F, E,G and E beads so the 2D sit side by side against the F bead (fig 37).

Pass the needle through the beads at the start of the rope and back through the connection to the 2D emerging from the first D bead (fig 38).

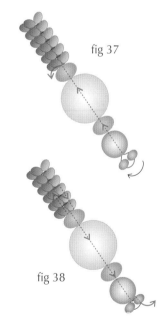

fig 37

fig 38

fig 39

fig 40

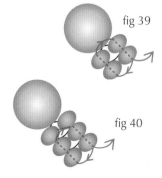

Thread on 2D. Pass down the second D of the first stitch, up through the first D of that stitch and the first D just added (fig 39).

Thread on 2D and pass down the second D of the previous stitch, the first D of that stitch and the first D of the new stitch (fig 40). Repeat until you have 25 rows of 2D in total.

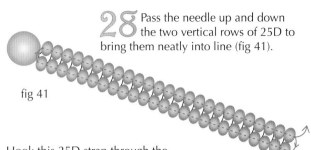

28 Pass the needle up and down the two vertical rows of 25D to bring them neatly into line (fig 41).

fig 41

Hook this 25D strap through the wire loop on the left-hand side of the branch and pass the needle through the F, E, G and E link beads to emerge at the base of the strap rope. Make several stitches backwards and forwards through these link beads to make the connections of the herringbone rope and the D bead connecting strap firm.

Finish off this thread end neatly and securely.

29 Repeat step 26 to make a new rope and work through step 27 until you have made 20 rows of 2D strap. Bring the D beads into line as fig 41.

The end of this D bead strap attaches directly to the branch at the base of the small bud branch made in step 23. Attach the last 2D of the strap to the fifth and sixth row rope beads immediately adjacent to the bud branch (fig 42).

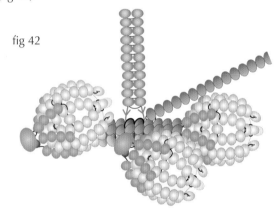

fig 42

Pass the needle back along the D bead strap to the F, E, G and E bead link so you can make the connection between this strap and the rope firm and secure as before. Leave the thread end loose for the moment.

30 Return to the end of the strap that will be on the right when the necklace is worn. Attach the needle to this thread end.

Try the necklace for size and add any additional rows of herringbone rope necessary to make this side of the necklace up to the desired length.

The Bead Tag - Thread on 1F, 1D, 1E, 1G, 1D and 3C. Leaving aside the last 3C to anchor the strand, pass the needle back through the previous 1D and the following beads just added to emerge at the end of the rope (fig 43).

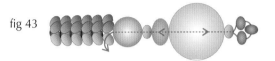

fig 43

Pass the needle into the last few rows of the rope and back through the tag beads just added to make the connection firm and the tag strong.

Finish off the thread end neatly and securely.

31 Attach the needle to the thread at the end of the other herringbone rope strap and make any necessary length adjustment as before.

The Bead Loop - Thread on 1F, 1E and sufficient D beads to make a loop that will just fit over the G bead of the bead tag (approximately 20D). Pass back through the E and F beads to draw up the loop and reinforce both the connection to the rope and the loop with several further thread passes.

Finish off the thread end neatly and securely.

32 To complete the design the E and H single row bud stalk made in step 23 needs to be attached to the D bead two-row strap.

Attach the needle to one of the thread ends behind the bud cluster on the right and pass up through 15D of the 2D strap along the edge adjacent to the bud stalk. Make sufficient square stitches to catch the E bead bud stalk to the D bead strap, and if necessary, the H bead stalk to the E bead stalk similarly.

Finish off all remaining thread ends.

Kyoto Inspiration
Akiko Brooch

The Brooch is Made in Six Stages

The two open blossoms and the large bud are made.
Two small buds are made.
The herringbone rope for the branch is made and threaded onto the hat pin.
The pin is bent to form the brooch mechanism.
The top of the branch is extended and the buds attached.
The lower end of the branch is extended and the open blossoms attached to complete the design.

33 The Blossoms and the Large Bud - Following steps 1 to 6 make the five petals of the first blossom.

Make the stamens as in step 7 using C beads for the main shafts and a single A bead at the top of each stamen.
Add 1F bead to the centre of the stamen ring as in step 8.

Repeat to make a second five-petal blossom to match.
Set aside for the moment.

Make one large bud as in steps 9 to 15 adding 1C in step 12 between the tips of the bud instead of a B bead.

Leave the thread ends loose and set aside.

Simple and elegant this brooch is so easy to wear.
This example is made in the pinky hues of the May-flowering hawthorn tree with its shiny burgundy bark.

decoration on brooch measures 6.5cm

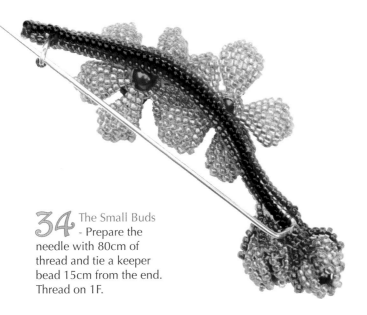

34 The Small Buds
- Prepare the needle with 80cm of thread and tie a keeper bead 15cm from the end. Thread on 1F.

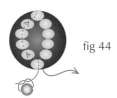

fig 44

Thread on 6A and pass through the F bead to make a strap on the side.

Pass through the first 1A and thread on 4A. Pass through the sixth A of the first strap and through the F bead to complete the first petal (fig 44).

Repeat to make three more petals around the F bead and add 1C to the top of the bud as in fig 24 to complete. Remove the needle and set aside.

Make one more bud to match.

35 The Herringbone Branch
- Referring to step 16 prepare the needle with 1.5m of single thread and tie a keeper bead 40cm from the end. Thread on 3C and 1D. Make the beads into a ring as fig 30. Make 3cm of herringbone rope. Read the Extra Info box below.

Extra Info....
You will need to thread the hat pin down the centre of this herringbone rope. If you work with a tight tension the central space might be too narrow to allow the pin to pass easily.

Test the pin for fit when you have 3cm of rope - if it's very tight you will need to work the rope with the pin *in situ*.

Working with the pin *in situ* - Start the rope again with the four-bead ring threaded onto the pin. Position the ring 15mm from the head-end. Work your stitches around the pin towards the point.

Continue working the herringbone rope until it measures 5cm long.

If you have worked your rope away from the pin you now need to thread the pin through the rope. Pass the pin from the keeper bead end to the needle end through the centre space. Stop when you have 15mm of pin showing at the keeper bead end.

36 Making the Brooch Mechanism
- The flat end of the pin is now converted into the catch for the brooch. Using round nosed pliers grip the pin against the back of the flat head - you need to make a 3mm wide bend so you will need to use the pliers quite close to the their tips.

Bend the wire to make a 3mm hook (fig 45).

8mm back along the pin you need to make a second bend - this will be very close to your beading. If necessary ease your beading along a bit and place the tips of the pliers in position.

Hold the pliers as in fig 46 with the hook to the side and the pin vertical.

fig 45   fig 46

Keep the pliers still and push the hooked end of the pin away from you to make a 90º bend. Ease the beading back up to the bend.

37
Return to the needle end of the rope. Place the tips of the pliers on the hat pin immediately adjacent to this end of the rope. You need to make a 90º bend to mirror the previous bend (see fig 47). Holding the pliers still use your fingers to bend the pin.

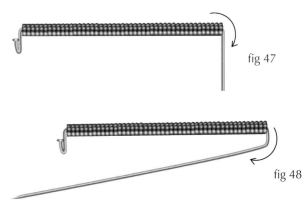

fig 47

fig 48

8mm along the pin hold the pin with the pliers - this time use the pliers closer to the hinge so you can make a more gradual curve in the wire. Hold the pliers still and bend the pointed end of the pin back towards the hook (fig 48). Make the bend to about 75º to give a spring to the mechanism.

fig 49

Catch the pin in the hook to check the alignment (fig 49).

Undo the catch and gently bend the front portion of the pin (covered by the herringbone rope) into a gentle curve (see photograph above). Catch the pin in the hook again and attach the pin guard.

38 Extending the Branch to Attach the Buds - Return to the needle end of the rope again. Although the bend in the pin has crossed over the edge of the last row of herringbone stitch you can still see the four beads of the row.

Work three rows of herringbone stitch rope to extend the stem away from the pin (fig 50). It will be fiddly to make the first row bridge over the bend in the pin but don't pull the thread too tight or the rope will 'waist'. Remove the needle.

fig 50

fig 51

39 Attach the needle to the long thread end of the first small bud made in step 34. Remove the keeper bead.

Pass the needle down the centre of the rope extension just made and out through a C bead of a convenient row to pull the bud up snugly to the end of the rope (fig 51).

Remove the needle and reattach it to the end of the rope.

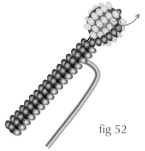
fig 52

40 Referring to step 19 you need to add four calyx straps to hold the small bud in place.

Thread on 6C.

Lay the strand between two petals on the small bud and square stitch the last C bead to the fourth or fifth A bead of the petals on either side (figs 52, 25 and 26).

Repeat to add three more calyx strands.

Pass down the main herringbone rope 7 or 8 rows and remove the needle.

41 The second small bud is supported on a separate short length of herringbone rope.

Prepare the needle with 1.5m of single thread and start the rope with a ring of 4C. Make six rows of rope.

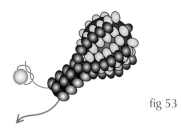
fig 53

Repeat step 39 to add the second small bud to the end of this rope (fig 53).

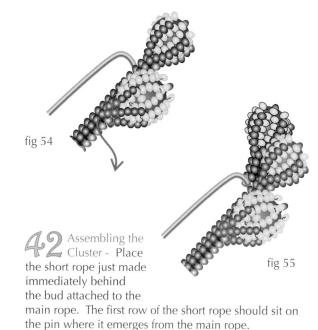
fig 54

fig 55

42 Assembling the Cluster - Place the short rope just made immediately behind the bud attached to the main rope. The first row of the short rope should sit on the pin where it emerges from the main rope.

The large bud needs to be attached to the front of the long rope just below the two small buds - hold the large bud in place. Does the arrangement work? Do you need to add more rows to the short herringbone rope or adjust the large bud position?

Make any necessary adjustments and stitch the cluster elements into place starting with the large bud.

Extend the calyx straps on the large bud to the main rope (fig 54).

Attach the end of the short rope to the back of the cluster making a stitch or two between the pin and the first row of the rope (fig 55).

Finally make a few neat stitches between all three buds to keep everything compact and neat.

43 Return to the start of the main rope. Remove the keeper bead and attach the needle.

Working from the ring made in step 35, extend the rope beyond the end of the pin by 3 to 5 rows (as fig 50).

Position the two blossoms on the main rope and stitch firmly into place. Finish off all remaining thread ends neatly and securely.

Sunflower Necklace

Sunshine

soaking through the golden petals of heavy, nodding sunflower heads and the hum of bees getting drunk on nectar.

Make the matching Honey Bee Earrings and think of the heat soaking through to your bones.

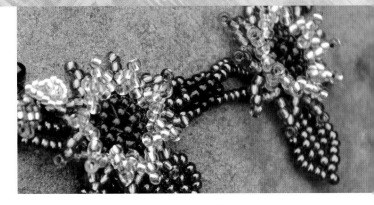

You Will Need

Materials for the Necklace

5g of size 10/0 silver lined brown seed beads A
5g of size 10/0 silver lined dark gold seed beads B
3g of size 10/0 silver lined gold seed beads C
6g of size 10/0 scarab green seed beads D
0.2g of size 15/0 silver lined gold seed beads F
0.2g of size 15/0 dark wine lined seed beads G
0.2g of size 15/0 silver lined crystal seed beads H
Two 4mm topaz fire polished faceted beads J
One 4mm black fire polished faceted bead K
One size 6/0 black seed bead L
0.2g of size 11/0 frost black seed beads M
Two 6mm topaz fire polished faceted beads N
Black size D beading thread

Tools

One size 13 and one size 10 beading needle
A pair of scissors to trim the threads

The Necklace is Made in Five Stages

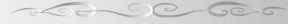

The three sunflowers are assembled first.
The leaves are made and attached to the flowers.
The flowers and leaves are linked together.
The side straps are added and the clasp created.
The bee is made and stitched into place.

1 The Sunflowers - Prepare the size 10 needle with 1.5m of single thread and tie a keeper bead 15cm from the end. Thread on 4A.

Pass the needle through the first bead again to bring the beads into a circle (fig 1).

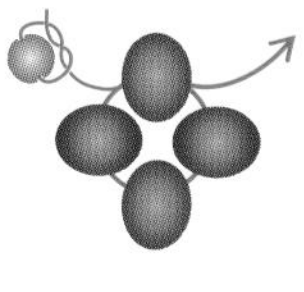

fig 1

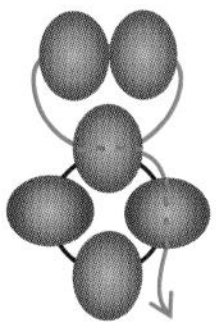

fig 2

2 Thread on 2A.

Pass the needle through the A bead on the circle once more and the following A bead (fig 2).

Repeat step 2 three times (fig 3).

fig 3

3 Pass the needle back through the first 2A beads added in step 2. Thread on 1A and pass through the following 2A (fig 4).

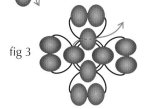

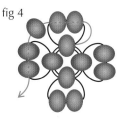

fig 4

Repeat three more times to add 4A in total to the edge of the work (fig 5).

fig 5

Pass the needle through the 12A beads of the last row to bring them close together - this may cup the centre of the disc a little.

Extra Info....

This technique is an adaptation of square stitch. The beads are added to the edge of the work as individual square stitches. The needle is then passed through the separate stitches to link the beads together and allow the work to be tightened without building up too much thread through the bead holes.

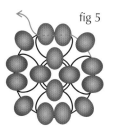

4 Thread on 2A and pass through the A bead on the edge of the disc and the following 1A (fig 6).

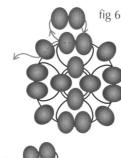

fig 6

Thread on 1A and pass through the new A bead on the edge of the disc and the following A bead (fig 7).

Repeat these two stitches to add alternate 2A and 1A to each of the A beads around the edge of the disc (see fig 8).

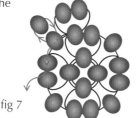
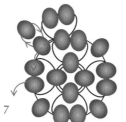

fig 7

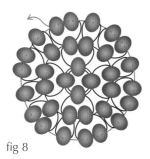

fig 8

Pass the needle through all of the beads just added to complete a row of 18A around the edge of the disc (fig 8).

Pull the thread quite firmly to reinforce the domed profile. The domed side of the disc will be the front of the flower.

5 The petals are made in two layers - a long layer is made first, followed by a shorter set of petals which overlays the first. All of the petals attach to the A beads around the edge of the cupped disc.

Referring to fig 9 thread on 5B.

Leaving aside the last bead to anchor the strand pass the needle down the fourth B bead in the opposite direction.

Thread on 3B. Pass the needle through the preceding A bead on the edge of the disc and the following 1A to position the petal across these 2A beads on the edge of the disc (fig 9).

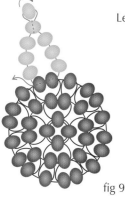

fig 9

6 Pass the needle through the next 2A around the disc edge and thread on 5B. Leave aside the last A bead to anchor the strand and pass back down the fourth A bead as before.

Thread on 2B.

Pass the needle down through the first B of the previous petal and the 2A beads at the base of this petal (fig 10).

Repeat step 6 six more times.

fig 10

7 The ninth petal links to both the first and eighth petals.

Pass the needle through the last 2A of the disc edge and up through the last B bead of the first petal. Thread on 4B and pass back through the third B just added to create the anchor.

Thread on 2B. Pass the needle down through the first B of the eighth petal and the 2A beads at the base of this petal as before.

Pass the needle through the next 1A bead around the disc edge. Make sure you are at the front of the domed central disc to start the second layer.

Extra Info....
The petals on the first layer link together through the shared B beads to make a smooth, uncluttered back to the flower.
The second, shorter C bead petals are all independent of one another - this makes them bunch a little to give a more ragged sunflower-like appearance to the finished flower.

8 Thread on 4C. Leaving aside the last C bead to form an anchor pass the needle down the third C bead.

Thread on 2C and pass the needle through the previous A bead on the edge of the disc and the following 1A (fig 11).

Pass through the next 2A around the disc and repeat eight times to complete nine petals.

Leave the thread ends attached and set aside.

Make two more flowers to match.

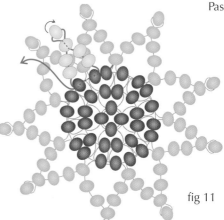

fig 11

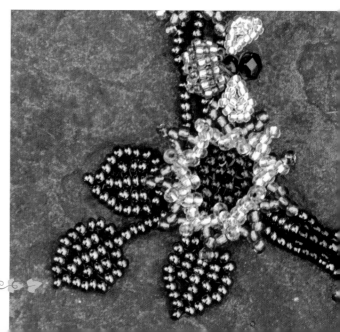

9 The Leaves - Turn the flowers onto their fronts and arrange so that one B bead petal on each flower points directly down to 6 o'clock (fig 12).

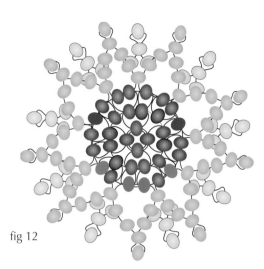

fig 12

In fig 12 the A beads marked in cerise will support the central dangling leaf on each flower.

The blue beads will support a further leaf on either side of the central flower only.

The purple beads will support the leaf links on either side of each flower.

Leave the flowers in a row, on their fronts, ready to add the leaves. The leaves are added to the back of the flowers.

10 Prepare the needle with 80cm of single thread and tie a keeper bead 15cm from the end. Thread on 13D.

Leaving aside the last 3D to anchor the strand pass the needle back through the tenth D bead and the following 5D to emerge between the fourth and fifth D beads of the 13D (fig 13).

Thread on 8D. Pass the needle through the 3D beads of the anchor to bring the new beads into an arch around the side of the main strand (fig 14).

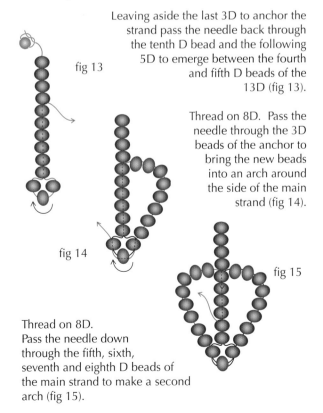

fig 13

fig 14

fig 15

Thread on 8D. Pass the needle down through the fifth, sixth, seventh and eighth D beads of the main strand to make a second arch (fig 15).

11 Thread on 3D. Pass the needle down through the sixth and seventh D beads of the main strand (fig 16).

Pass the needle up through the second and third D beads of the 3D just added.

Pass down through the sixth and fifth D beads of the second arch and up through the last 2D of the 3D a second time (fig 17).

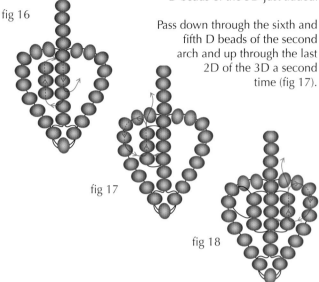

fig 16

fig 17

fig 18

12 Pass the needle down through the sixth, seventh and eighth D beads of the main strand and make a matching 3D link to the first arch (fig18).

Pass the needle up through the top 5D beads of the main strand to emerge adjacent to the keeper bead.

13 Return to the left-hand flower from step 9 and pass the needle through the A bead marked purple on the left of the flower disc.

Pass the needle back down the beads of the leaf stalk and pull to bring the end of the stalk up snug to the edge of the disc. Finish off the thread neatly and securely between the beads of the leaf without blocking the holes at the tip of the motif.

Remove the keeper bead. Attach the needle to this end and use it to reinforce the link to the purple bead on the flower. Finish off this thread end similarly.

14 Repeat steps 10 to 12 to make a second leaf.

Attach this leaf, in a similar manner, to the two cerise beads at the bottom of the left hand flower.

Make a further two leaves for the right-hand flower. Attach one to the purple bead on the right of the flower disc and one to the cerise beads at the bottom of the disc.

15 Make a fifth leaf. When the needle emerges alongside the keeper bead thread on 6D to extend the length of the stalk.

Attach this leaf to the two cerise beads marked on the back of the central flower.

Make a sixth and a seventh leaf - do not extend the stalks on these two leaves but attach one to each of the beads marked blue on the disc at the back of the central flower (see fig 12).

16 Linking the Flowers - Prepare the needle with 80cm of single thread and tie a keeper bead 15cm from the end.

Pass the needle through the bead marked purple on the left of the middle flower to point towards the flower on the left. Thread on 7D, 3A and 7D.

Pass the needle through the bead marked purple on the right of the left-hand flower. Pass the needle back through the last 7D and 3A added.

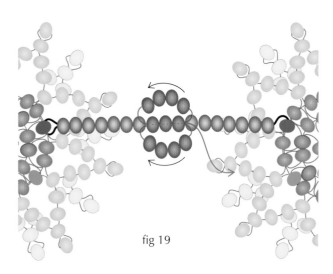

fig 19

Thread on 4A and pass through the 3A on the main row once more. Thread on 4A and repeat to create a loop on either side of the 3A beads (fig 19).

Pass the needle through the remaining 7D of the strand.

Pass the needle through the purple bead on the edge of the middle flower disc and the next A bead around the disc.

17 Thread on 8D. Pass the needle through the middle 2A of one of the 4A loops at the centre of the first strand (fig 20).

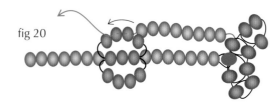

fig 20

Thread on 8D. Pass the needle through the corresponding A bead on the edge of the left-hand flower disc to bring this strand parallel to the first.

18 Reposition the needle to emerge from the A bead at the other side of the purple A bead on the edge of the disc (see fig 21).

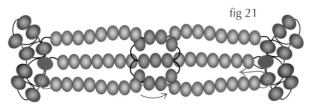

fig 21

Repeat step 17 to complete a matching row on the other side of the original strand (fig 21).

Repeat steps 17 and 18 on the other side of the middle flower to make a matching link to the flower on the right.

Finish off all remaining thread ends neatly and securely.

19 The Side Straps - Prepare the needle with 1.2m of single thread and tie a keeper bead 15cm from the end. Thread on 11D.

Leaving aside the last 3D beads to anchor the strand, pass the needle back through the eighth D bead threaded and the following 5D to emerge from the gap between the second and third D beads (fig 22).

This starts a new leaf motif. Follow figs 14 to 18 to complete the motif - note the new leaf will have a 2D stalk not 4D as in figs 14 to 18.

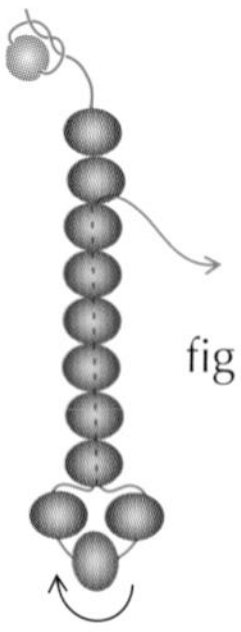

fig 22

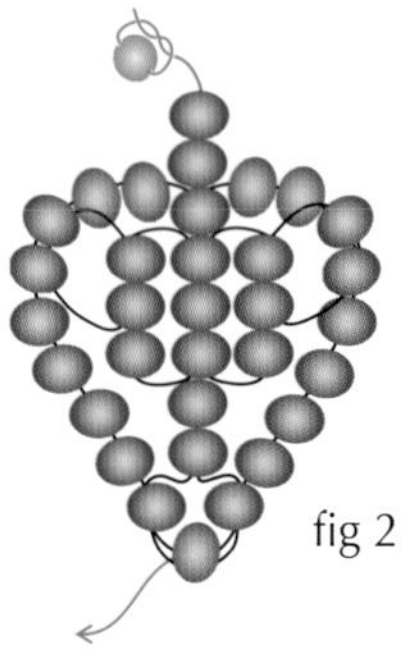

Pass the needle through the beads of the central stalk to emerge from the D bead at the tip of the anchor (fig 23).

fig 23

20 Thread on 1B, 1A, 1J, 1A, 1B and pass the needle through the end D bead of the leaf on the side of the right-hand flower.

fig 24

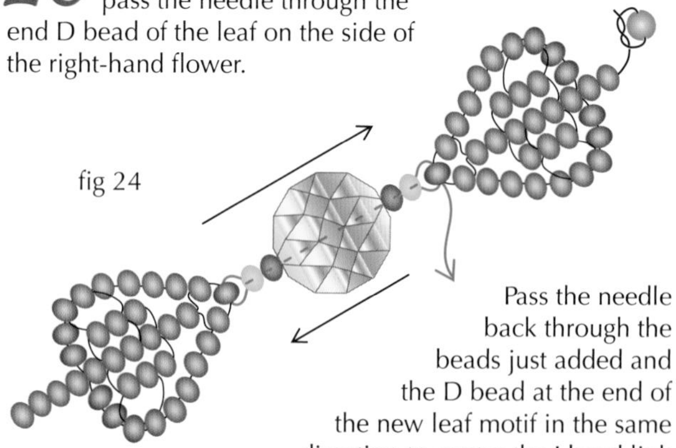

Pass the needle back through the beads just added and the D bead at the end of the new leaf motif in the same direction to centre the J bead link on the end of the leaf (fig 24).

Pass the needle through the D beads of the new leaf to emerge at the end of the stalk alongside the keeper bead.

Thread on 1B, 3A, 1B and 8D. Repeat the sequence until this side of the necklace reaches the desired length.

21 Thread on 1N, 1D, 1B, 1D, 1N, 1D and 3B. Leaving aside the last 3B beads to anchor the strand pass the needle back through the last D bead threaded and the following five beads (fig 25).

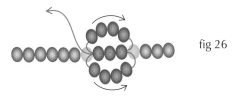

fig 25

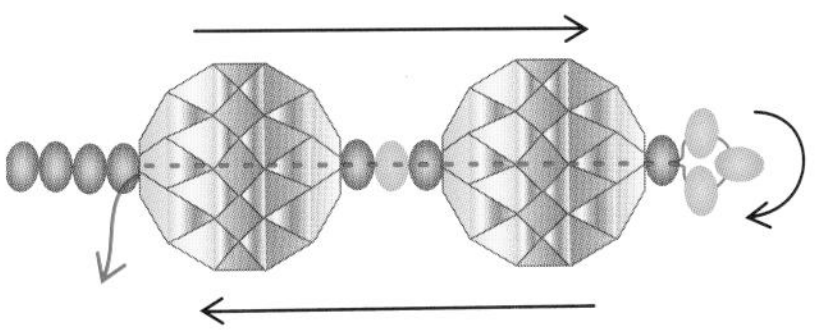

22 Pass the needle through the beads of the strap to emerge from the third A bead you encounter. Thread on 4A. Pass the needle through the previous 3A beads of the strap again to bring the 4A into a loop on the side of the main strand. Thread on 4A and repeat (fig 26).

fig 26

Pass the needle through the following 1B, 8D, 1B and 3A. Repeat until the needle reaches the keeper bead.

Strengthen the strap by passing the needle through the leaf and bead link to the centrepiece, back up the main strap, through the beads of the end tag and back down to the keeper bead again.

Finish off both thread ends neatly and securely.

23 Repeat steps 19 and 20 to start the second side strap on the other side of the centrepiece.

Thread on 1B, 1A and 1B followed by sufficient D beads to make a loop that will just fit over the N beads at the end of the other strap (approximately 16D). Pass the needle back down the 1B, 1A and 1B beads to draw up the loop.

Work the needle back down the remaining beads of the strap adding 4A bead loops to the 3A sections on the strap to match the other side of the necklace.

Strengthen the strap as before and finish off the remaining thread ends neatly and securely.

24 The Bee - Prepare the size 13 needle with 1.2m of single thread and tie a keeper bead 15cm from the end.

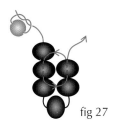

Thread on 6M.

Pass the needle through the second of the 6M beads in the same direction as before. Pass through the sixth M bead again to make a square stitch which brings these 2M beads parallel to one another (fig 27).

fig 27

Thread on 1M, 1L and 1K.

Pass the needle back down the L bead in the opposite direction and through the first 3M of the 6M (fig 28).

Note the orientation of the K and L beads just added. Referring to fig 28 the L bead should sit flat across the top of the two M bead columns. The K bead should sit across the top of the L bead with the hole at 90º to the holes in the L and M beads.

fig 28

fig 29

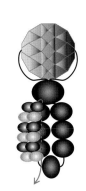

25 Thread on 1F, 1G, 1F, 1G, 1F and 1G.

Pass the needle down the 3M of the first column of M beads once more to bring the new beads into a strap (fig 29).

Repeat to make a second strap (fig 30). Make one more strap to match.

fig 30

26 Pass the needle through the horizontal M bead at the bottom of the two columns and up the second 3M column.

Make a further three straps of 1G, 1F, 1G, 1F, 1G and 1F on this column of 3M.

Push all the straps together so they cover the two widths of the columns (fig 31).

fig 31

The straps now need to be linked to one another to line up the F and G beads into horizontal stripes.

27 Referring to fig 32 pass the needle down through the first four beads of the last (sixth) strap to emerge from an F bead.

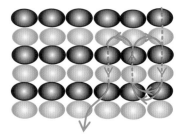

fig 32

Pass up the middle F and G beads of the fifth strap and back down through the middle G and F beads on the sixth strap.

Pass up the F and G beads of the fifth strap and down the G and F beads of the fourth strap (fig 32).

This has created a link between the sixth and fifth straps and lined up the F and G beads across the gap between the straps.

Repeat between the fifth and fourth straps; the fourth and third straps; the third and second straps and the second and first straps.

Pass the needle down through the M beads of the first column and up the second column to emerge between the L bead and the K bead.

28 Thread on 14H.

Pass the needle through the first H bead in the opposite direction to pull the other 13H into a loop.

Pass the needle up through the L bead (fig 33).

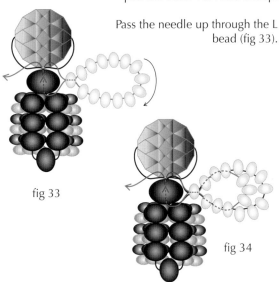

fig 33

fig 34

29 Pass the needle through the first H bead of the wing and the following 3H on one side of the wing loop.

Thread on 3H and pass the needle back towards the first H bead through the last 3H beads on the other side of the wing loop. Pass the needle through the first H bead and up the L bead (fig 34).

Repeat to make a second wing on the other side of the bee.

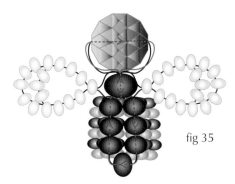

fig 35

30 To reinforce the head position pass the needle down and up the M bead columns; up through the L bead and through the K bead. Pass back down the L and M beads (fig 35).

31 Use the end of the thread to stitch the bee to the link between the middle flower and one of the side flowers.

Finish off all remaining thread ends neatly and securely.

Honey Bee Earrings

◦ ⤳ You Will Need ⤳ ◦

1g of size 10/0 silver lined brown seed beads A
2g of size 15/0 silver lined gold seed beads F
0.8g of size 15/0 dark wine lined seed beads G
0.8g of size 15/0 silver lined crystal seed beads H
Four 4mm black fire polished faceted beads K
Four size 6/0 black seed beads L
0.8g of size 11/0 frost black seed beads M
40cm of 7 strand 0.010 fine stranded beading wire
Six silver-plated French crimps
A pair of silver-plated earfittings
Black size D beading thread

Tools
A pair of flat-faced pliers

The Earrings are Made in Three Stages

The four bees are assembled first.
The sunflower motifs are made next.
The bees are attached to the flowers and the earfittings added to complete the design.

32 The Bees - Following steps 24 to 30 make four bee motifs.

Finish the thread ends on each bee neatly and securely without blocking the holes in the K beads.

33 The Flowers - Using a size 13 needle and 1m of single thread work steps 1, 2 and 3 to make a central disc for the flower. The petals will attach to the A beads around the edge of this disc - one petal on each A bead.

34 Thread on 4F.

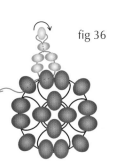

fig 36

Leaving aside the last 1F to anchor the strand pass the needle back through the third F bead in the opposite direction.

Thread on 2F. Pass the needle through the single A bead on the disc edge to position the petal astride the A bead.

Pass through the next A bead around the edge (fig 36).

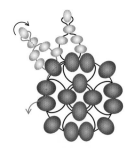

fig 37

35 Thread on 4F. As before pass the needle back down the third F bead threaded to bring the fourth F bead into an anchor.

Thread on 1F.

Pass the needle through the first F bead of the previous petal; the A bead on the edge where the needle emerged at the end of step 33 and the following 1F bead (fig 37).

Repeat step 34 to add nine more petals to the flower.

36 The twelfth petal links to both the first and the eleventh petals.

Pass the needle through the last F bead of the first petal and thread on 3F.

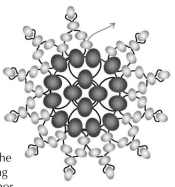

fig 38

Pass the needle back down the second of the new 3F to bring the third F bead into an anchor. Thread on 1F and complete the petal as before.

Finish off the thread ends neatly and securely without blocking the holes at the tips of the petals and make a second flower to match.

37 Assembling the Earring - Cut the fine stranded beading wire in half.

Referring to fig 39 pass the ends of the first wire, in opposite directions, through the end F beads of two adjacent petals.

Pass the two ends of the wire across the back of the flower and through the F beads at the ends of the two petals on the opposite side of the flower - note that the ends of the wire come towards one another through the second 2F beads.

Pass both ends through one French crimp so that the wire ends emerge parallel to one another (fig 39).

If necessary adjust the wire so the two ends dangling from the flower are approximately the same length as one another.

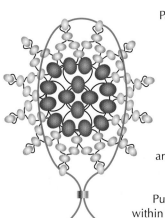

fig 39

Push the French crimp up to within 4-6mm of the edge of the flower - make sure the flower is not being pulled out of shape by the beading wire. Secure the crimp by squashing flat onto the wire with a pair of flat-nosed pliers.

38 Thread one French crimp and the H bead at the top of the first bee onto one end of the wire.

Pass the end of the wire back up through the French crimp so that the bee dangles from the loop created in the wire (fig 40). Ensure the best side of both the bee and the flower are to the front but do not secure the crimp yet.

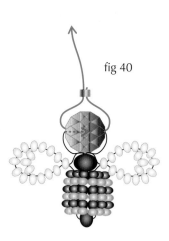

fig 40

Repeat with a second bee and the other end of the wire. Adjust the lengths of the wires by easing them through the crimps to varying degrees until you are happy with the position of the bees below the flower.

Push the crimps up as close to the H beads as you can without compromising the way the bees swing from the loops created in the wire. Squash the crimps flat and trim the excess wire as close as you can to the crimps.

Repeat with the remaining flower and two bees to make the second earring mirror the first.

Attach the earfittings to the wire passing between the top petals to complete the design.

Bouquet Necklace

Simple stitches can build beautiful things. This stunning necklace is surprisingly easy to make.

A plaited wire
ribbon makes an ideal base
for a collage of beaded flowers,
lucite flowers, leaves and
glass blossoms.

Use all your favourite colours, or seed beads
leftover from previous projects. Choose a few
feature beads for contrasting texture and a foliage
colour to bring it all together.

For a more contemporary look swap the
beaded rope straps for a chunky chain or a
velvet ribbon.

necklace length 47cm

This is an ideal project to use all of your favourite floral seed bead colours. Beads A to D in this recipe should be colour matched to tone with your selection.

The Necklace is Made in Four Stages

The knitted wire support for the centrepiece is made first.
The seed bead flowers are made in a variety of sizes.
The collage of flowers and leaves is assembled.
The side straps are made and attached to complete the necklace.

39 Making the Wire Support - Fold the knitted wire in half all the way along the length. Open out this fold and fold both long edges into the centre crease. Remake the centre crease so the edges of the ribbon are tucked on the inside (fig 41).

Gently start to stretch the ribbon lengthwise. Making sure you maintain the folds, work end to end easing out the length. It will increase to approximately 1.4m long, it will decrease in width to 7-8mm and become sinuously tough.

fig 41

40 Cut off one third of the stretched ribbon length. Put the shorter piece to the side for the moment.

41 Cut off one third of the remaining long length to give you two pieces - one twice as long as the other.

Referring to fig 42 make a 25mm diameter loop in the centre of the long length. Tuck the end of the short length inside the crossover so it is neatly concealed and pin into place. This gives you three ends to plait.

fig 42

fig 43

Plait the three ribbons to make a flat firm braid. Bend the longest end into a loop to match the loop at the other end.

Keeping the flat profile of the braid, trim and tuck the other ends into the base of the new loop and pin in place (fig 43).

Use a doubled ash-coloured thread and discreet small stitches secure the loops and the cut ribbon ends. Remove the pins.

Repeat step 41 with the short ribbon length from step 40.

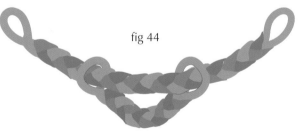

fig 44

42 Thread the long ribbon through the loops of the short ribbon positioning the short length at the centre of the longer length. Ease the long ribbon into a flat curve and move both ends of the short ribbon in towards the centre to create a lower curve (fig 44).

Secure the short ribbon with a few stitches as before. The support for the collage is complete.

43 Making the Flowers -
Following the techniques
shown in steps 1 to 8 and using your
flower colour seed beads make an assortment of sunflower motifs:-

Make the first flower with the same bead counts as in steps
1 to 8.

Make the second flower with the same bead count for the
flower centre but with longer petals - six beads for the outer
layer of petals and five beads for the inner layer.

Make the third flower with even longer petals - seven seed
beads for the outer layer and six beads for the inner layer.

For a small flower make the centre following steps 1 to 3.
Add two layers of six petals, the outer layer using five seed
beads and four seed beads for the inner layer.

Repeat until you have sufficient flowers to cover 75% of
the wire plait centrepiece. Arrange the finished motifs, the
lucite flowers and leaves in the approximate finished positions and take a photo to remind yourself of the layout.

44 Assembling the
Centrepiece Collage -
Start with one of the larger seed
bead flowers.

Remove the keeper bead and
attach the needle to the short
thread end.

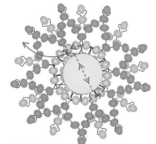

fig 45

Use this thread end to stitch a toning E bead in the centre of
the flower on the reverse of the motif (fig 45). This
pushes the central dome of the flower forward, makes the
motif much more rigid and therefore easier to stitch into
place. Finish off this thread end.

45 Attach the needle to the other thread end. Make
small stab stitches to attach the seed beads around
the edge of the flower centre to the plaited wire support.
Finish off the thread end.

Repeat steps 44 and 45 to add the remainder of the seed
bead flowers.

Using a doubled thread and few extra seed beads, add the
glass flowers, lucite flowers and leaves in the gaps.

46 The Side Straps - Prepare the needle
with 1.5m of single ash-coloured
thread and tie a keeper bead 15cm from the
end.
Thread on 3A and 1B. Pass the needle through
the first A bead to make a ring (fig 46).

fig 46

Using this ring as the base for a four-bead herringbone
stitch rope, work sufficient rows of 2A, and 1A and 1B for
the first side strap. The B beads should form a continuous
line along one edge of the rope.

47 Thread on 1F and a suitable bead combination to
make the bead tag for the clasp.

Pass the needle back through the F bead and the A bead on
the diagonally opposite side to the B bead at the end of the
rope. The A beads along this edge are embellished with a
contrast row.

Thread on 1C and square stitch to
the next A bead along (fig 47).

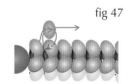

fig 47

48 Make two 1C stitches
(fig 48).

Make one stitch with 1D.

Make three C bead
stitches.

fig 48

Make the next stitch
with 1D and 1C
(fig 49).

fig 49

This increase
stitch shapes the
rope into a gentle
curve.

Repeat step 48 until you reach the start of the rope.
Making sure the rope is curving in the correct direction,
stitch it securely to the looped end of the wire centrepiece.

Repeat from step 46 to make the second side strap adding
an appropriate size bead loop at the centre-back to
complete the clasp.

Bluebell Wood
Necklace & Earrings

necklace measures 39cm

Ripples

of velvety bluebells carpet the springtime woods. Pale fingers of dappled sunlight caress the stems as the delicate bells shyly turn their heads to the floor. The necklace shows two arched stems, back-to-back with dainty earrings to match. A bolder interpretation can be seen on page 73.

You Will Need

To Make the Necklace

5g of size 10/0 green lined topaz seed beads A
7g of size 15/0 frost opaque blue AB seed beads B
Nine 6mm blue velvet glass round beads C
Ten 4mm blue velvet glass round beads D
Seventeen 3mm gold metallic round beads E
Twelve 2.5mm gold metallic round beads F
Navy blue size D beading thread

To Make the Earrings

1.5g of size 10/0 green lined topaz seed beads A
2g of size 15/0 frost opaque blue AB seed beads B
Six 4mm blue velvet glass round beads D
Eight 2.5mm gold metallic round beads F
Eight 4mm scarab blue faceted crystal rounds G
A pair of gilt earfittings
Two 4mm gilt soldered jump rings

Tools

A size 13 beading needle
A pair of scissors to trim the threads
A pair of pliers to attach the earfittings

The Necklace is Made in Five Stages

The first few stitches establish the foundation rows across the bottom of the central V. The central V will be worked upwards from these foundation rows in two halves.

The flower buds of the first half are made as the first stem is developed.

The central flower is added to the bottom of the foundation.

The opposite stem is made to complete the V.

The side straps are added to complete the design.

Extra Info....

Most of the stitching in this chapter is based on square stitch where the thread follows a square path to bring the beads into line.

The thread builds up quite quickly in the bead holes adding firmness and structure to the work. It is important not to tie any knots or finish any thread ends, until instructed to do so, as these can easily block the path of the needle.

---

1 The Foundation Rows - Prepare the needle with 1.5m of single thread and tie a keeper bead 15cm from the end.

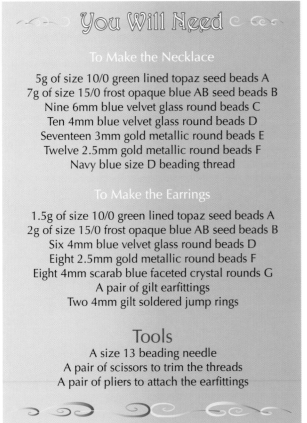

Thread on 3A.

Pass the needle back through the first A bead to bring the second and third beads flat against the first (fig 1).

2 Thread on 2A. Pass down the previous 2A and up the new 2A to bring the new beads alongside (fig 2).

Thread on 2A. Pass up the previous 2A and down the new beads to make a new column of 2A (fig 3).

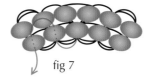

3 Pass up the lower A bead of the previous column, down the lower A of the new column and back up the previous A (fig 4).

Pass down the first A from step 1 (fig 5).

Repeat figs 2, 3 and 4 on the other side of the first 3A beads to add two columns of 2A. Pass the needle back down the first A bead to complete a symmetrical arch (fig 6).

Pass the needle up and down the lower 2A just added to be in the correct position to start the first flower bud (fig 7).

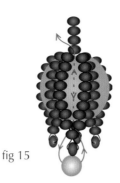

4 The Large Flower Bud - Thread on 4A, 5B, 1C and 7B. Pass the needle through the C bead again to make a strap on the side of the C bead (fig 8). Thread on 7B and pass through the C bead again to make a second strap.

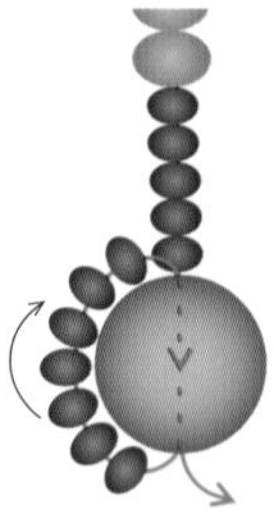

Repeat six more times to make eight straps of 7B in total - make sure the straps do not snag, or cross over one another.

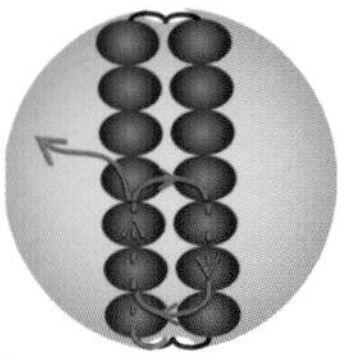

fig 8

fig 9

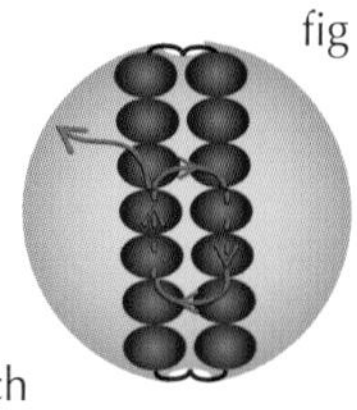

fig 10

fig 11

5 Referring to fig 9 (which shows two adjacent straps) pass the needle up through the first 3B of the first strap.

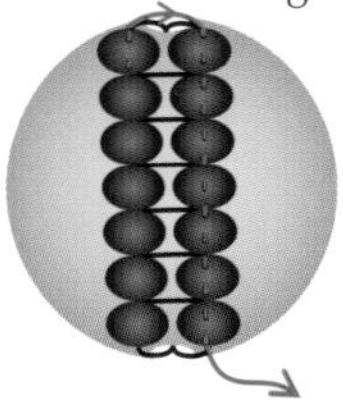

Pass down the third and second B of the adjacent strap and up the second and third B of the first strap to make a square stitch (fig 9).

Referring to fig 10 pass up through the following 1B and repeat the square stitch.

Repeat twice more, moving up the first row 1B at a time, to link the two straps together and emerge from the sixth B of the first strap. Pass up the following 1B and down the 7B of the adjacent strap (fig 11).

6 Thread on 3B.

Leaving aside the last B bead to anchor the strand pass back through the previous 1B (fig 12).

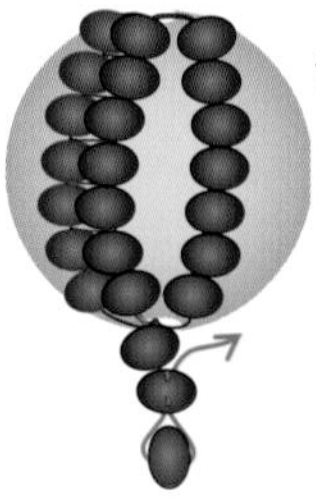

fig 12

Thread on 1B and pass the needle up through the first 3B of the next 7B single strap around the C bead (fig 13).

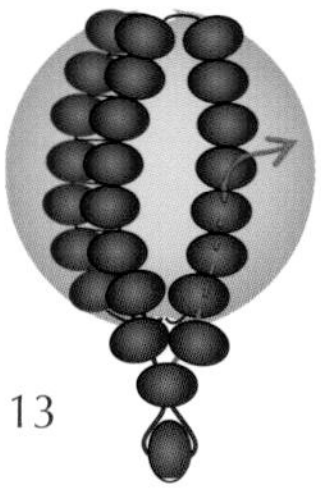

You have made the first petal tip.

fig 13

7 Repeat step 5 to link the current 7B single strap to the next 7B single strap around the C bead, and step 6 to add a petal tip link to the next 7B single strap around the C bead.

Repeat steps 5 and 6 twice more to make two more pairs of straps and two more petal tips.

Pass the needle to the top of the current strap (fig 14).

fig 14

8 Pass the needle down through the C bead to emerge between the petal tips just made.

Thread on 1E and pass back through the C bead to pull the E bead up close to the C bead (fig 15). Make sure the thread does not snag on the petal tips.

fig 15

9 Pass the needle up through the following 5B and 4A to the bottom edge of the foundation rows. Pass up through the next 2A along this edge of the foundation rows.

Referring to fig 16 thread on 2A. Pass down the adjacent A bead along the top of the foundation rows and up through the previous foundation bead and the first A of the 2A just added.

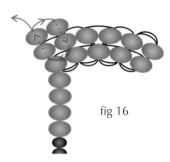

fig 16

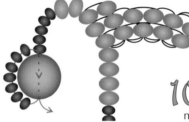

fig 17

10 Thread on 2A, 5B, 1C and 7B. Pass the needle down through the C bead to make a strap on the side (fig 17). This starts the new large flower bud.

Referring to step 4 make seven more straps of 7B to cover the C bead.

Repeat steps 5 to 8 to complete the flower bud as before.

11 Referring to fig 18 pass the needle through the 5B and 2A above the flower bud and the following 1A of the foundation.

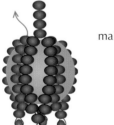

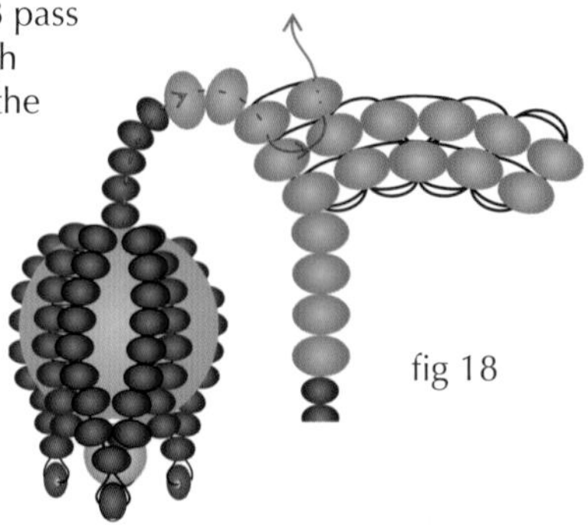

fig 18

Pass up through the adjacent 1A.
If necessary adjust the tension in the thread so the 2A and 5B connection to the bud forms a neat arch allowing the flower head to nod downwards.

12 Referring to fig 19 thread on 1A and pass down through the next A along the top of the foundation. Pass up through the adjacent 1A and the A bead above it to make a square stitch.

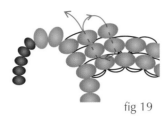

fig 19

These two columns of A beads are now extended to start the main stem for this side of the necklace.

Thread on 2A and referring to fig 20 square stitch to the top of the two A bead columns (fig 20).

fig 20

Repeat this 2A stitch four times to extend the stem to six rows above the foundation (fig 21).

The stem is now made wider with the addition of a third column.

fig 21

13 Referring to fig 22 pass the needle down the second A of the previous 2A stitch and thread on 1A.

fig 22

Pass down the previous A again to bring the new A bead alongside it with the holes parallel.

The stem is now worked across these 3A beads for the next three rows.

Reposition the needle by passing up through the first A bead of the 3A row (fig 23).

fig 23

14 Thread on 2A and square stitch to the first 2A of the previous row (fig 24).

fig 24

To add the last bead of the row refer to fig 25 and pass the needle down the top 2A of the second column and up the single A of the third. Thread on 1A and pass down the top 2A of the second column again to draw the new A bead into position as the final bead of the row.

Reposition the needle by passing up through the top 2A of the first column (fig 26).

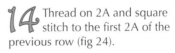

fig 25

fig 26

Repeat step 14 twice more to complete four rows of 3A (see fig 27).

15 Repeat steps 10 and 11 to add a new large flower bud and position the needle for the next stem section (fig 27).

As before, adjust the tension in the thread so the 2A and 5B connection to the bud forms a neat arch allowing the flower head to nod downwards.

Repeating the techniques shown in steps 12 to 14, add four rows of 2A stem and four rows of 3A stem.

The needle is now in the correct position to add the first small flower bud.

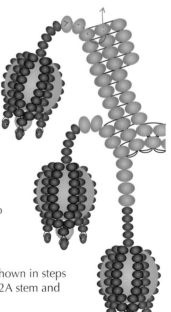

fig 27

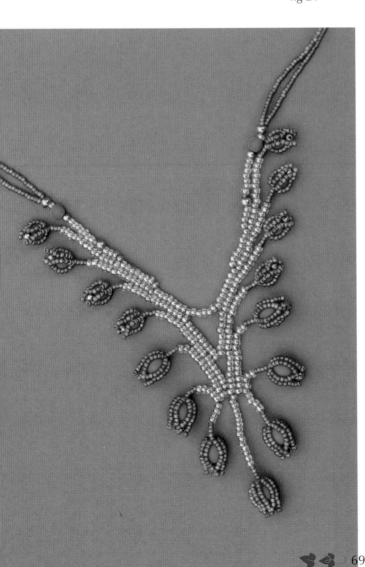

16 The Small Flower Bud - Thread on 2A, 5B, 1D and 5B. Pass the needle through the D bead again to make a strap on the side (fig 28).

Thread on 5B and pass through the D bead again to make a second strap. Repeat four times to make six straps in total.

These straps are now linked together with square stitches and petal tips as before.

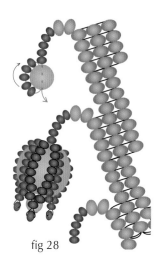

fig 28

17 Pass the needle through the first 3B of the first strap, down the adjacent third and second B of the adjacent strap and up the second and third B of the first strap (fig 29).

fig 29   fig 30   fig 31

Pass through the next 1B and repeat the square stitch to link the third and fourth B beads on this strap to the fourth and third B on the adjacent strap (fig 30).

Pass the needle through the fifth B of the first strap and down through the 5B of the adjacent strap (fig 31).

18 Add a petal tip between this strap and the next strap around the D bead as in step 6 (figs 32 and 33). The needle will be in the correct position to make the first square stitch between the new (third) strap and the fourth.

fig 32

fig 33

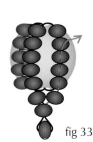

Repeat steps 17 and 18 to link the straps into pairs and add two further petal tips.

Finish with the needle emerging from the top of the first strap (fig 34).

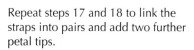

fig 34

fig 35

19 Pass the needle down through the D bead and thread on 1F.

Pass the needle back up through the D bead to pull the F bead up to the D bead and between the petal tips (fig 35).

20 Pass the needle up through the following 5B and 2A, the 1A of the main stem and up the adjacent A of the next stem column ready to begin the next stem section (fig 36).

As before check the tension in the thread to make sure the new flower bud is properly aligned.

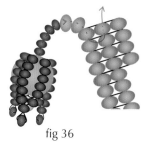

fig 36

*Repeat steps 12 to 14 to add four rows of 2A stem and four rows of 3A stem.

Repeat steps 16 to 19 to add a small flower bud and reposition the needle as in fig 36.

Repeat from * to fig 36 to add one more section of main stem and a third small flower bud.

White lined seed bead petals encase pale lilac pearls to make an exquisitely delicate necklace.

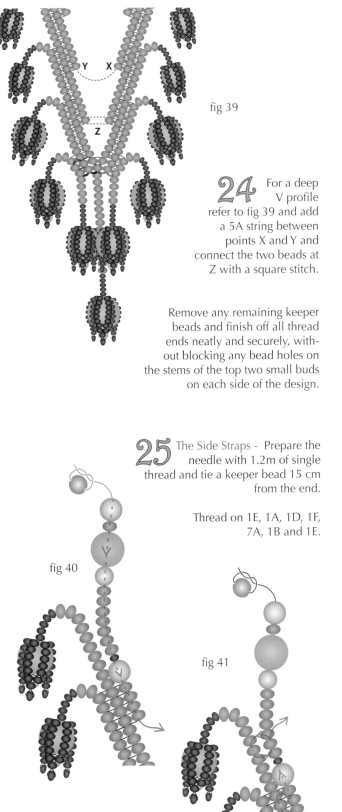

21 Thread on 8A to extend the main stem and repeat steps 16 to 19 to add the final small flower bud on this side of the design.

Referring to fig 37 pass the needle down the stem beads to emerge from the central A bead along the bottom edge of the foundation rows.

The central large flower bud hangs from this position.

fig 37

fig 38

fig 39

24 For a deep V profile refer to fig 39 and add a 5A string between points X and Y and connect the two beads at Z with a square stitch.

Remove any remaining keeper beads and finish off all thread ends neatly and securely, without blocking any bead holes on the stems of the top two small buds on each side of the design.

22 The Central Flower - Thread on 11A to extend the stem length and repeat steps 4 to 8 to complete the bud (see fig 38).

Pass the needle to the top of the stem.

Referring to fig 38 reposition the needle to emerge from the lower edge of the last foundation column.

This is the correct position to begin the first bud on this side of the design.

25 The Side Straps - Prepare the needle with 1.2m of single thread and tie a keeper bead 15 cm from the end.

Thread on 1E, 1A, 1D, 1F, 7A, 1B and 1E.

fig 40

fig 41

23 Repeat from step 4 to step 21 to make a mirror image set of buds and stems to complete a V-shaped centrepiece.

Before you finish off the thread ends compare the photos on pages 69 and 70.

The blue necklace on page 69 has a deep V profile, maintained by two links across the centre front of the V. The white necklace on page 70 has a wider, more open profile.

If you prefer the deeper V profile, you need to add two more stitches.

Pass the needle down through the exposed 4A stem section just below the last bud worked on the centrepiece (fig 40).

Referring to fig 41 pass the needle up through 3A of the adjacent stem column, the top A of the 4A section and the following 1E, 1B and 2A.

Square stitch this A bead to the fifth A bead of the stem supporting the top bud (fig 41). Pass the needle up through the following 5A, 1F, 1D, 1A and 1E to emerge alongside the keeper bead.

26 Thread on 45B, 1A, 1E, 1A, 50B, 1A, 1E and 1A. Now thread on sufficient B beads to make this side of the necklace up to your desired finished length - make a note of this number.

27 The Bead Tag - Thread on 1A, 1E, 1A, 1C, 1A, 1F, 1A, 1C, 1A, 1F and 3B. Leaving aside the last 3B to anchor the strand pass the needle back through the last F bead and the following nine beads to emerge just before the last stretch of B beads (fig 42).

fig 42

28 Thread on the same number of B beads as noted in step 26 to bring the needle back to the previous 1A, 1E and 1A beads. Pass the needle through these three beads (fig 43) and thread on 50B.

Pass the needle through the next 1A, 1E and 1A (as fig 43) and thread on 45B.

fig 43

Pass down through the beads added in step 25 and the 4A of the stem to emerge as fig 40.

Turn the needle as in fig 41 and pass back up through the beads of the first strand of the strap, through the beads of the tag (as fig 42) and through the beads of the second strand of the strap to emerge at the keeper bead. Remove the keeper bead and finish off both thread ends neatly and securely.

29 Repeat steps 25 and 26 on the other side of the centre front V. This strap will need a bead loop at the centre back.

Thread on 1A, 1E, 1A and sufficient B beads to make a loop that will just fit over the C beads of the tag (approximately 22B).

Pass the needle back through the 1A, 1E and 1A beads to draw up the loop.

Repeat step 28 to make the second strand of the strap and to reinforce the strands and the bead loop just made.

Finish off all remaining thread ends neatly and securely.

30 Prepare the needle with 1.5m of single thread and thread on 3A. Pass the needle through the first A bead in the same direction to bring the beads into a tight ring (fig 44).

fig 44

Thread on 3A, 1B, 1G, 1A, 1D and 5B. Pass the needle through the D bead again to make a strap on the side. This starts the first small bud.

Complete the bud with five more straps of 5B following steps 17 to 19.

31 Pass the needle up through the 1A, 1G, 1B and 4A above the bud to emerge from the A bead on the ring (fig 45).

fig 45

Thread on 11A, 1B, 1G, 1A, 1D and 5B. Pass the needle through the D bead again to make a strap on the side. This starts the second small bud.
Complete the bud as before and pass the needle back up the 11A and through the same A bead on the ring.

fig 46

32 Pass the needle through the following 2A of the ring (fig 46) and thread on 22A, 1B, 1G, 1A, 1D and 5B. Pass the needle through the D bead again to make a strap on the side. This starts the third small bud.

Complete the bud as before and pass the needle back up the 22A and the following 1A of the ring.

33 Thread on 1B, 1F, 1G and 1A. Pass the needle through a soldered jump ring. Pass the needle back down the 1A, 1G and 1F beads (see fig 47).

Thread on 1B and pass through the same A bead on the ring (fig 47).

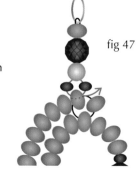

fig 47

Pass the needle through the connection to the jump ring twice more to make secure and finish off the thread ends neatly and securely.

Add an earfitting to the jump ring and repeat to make the second earring.

Dovedale Necklace

Bolder than the delicate Bluebell Wood Necklace, with additional buds and crystal tassel strands, this design suits longer length side straps.

necklace measures 52cm
plus 10cm of tassel strands

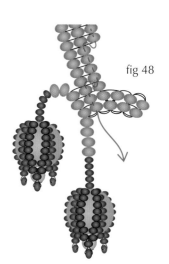

34 The Necklace Centre - Work steps 1 to 20 inclusive.

Referring to step 21 extend the main stem by 6A instead of 8A and add the final small flower to this side of the design.

Pass the needle down the stem beads as in fig 37 making an additional weave across the rows to emerge adjacent to the first flower bud on the lower edge of the foundation (fig 48).

fig 48

35 The Centre Front Flower and Crystal Strands - Thread on 14A, 5B, 1C and 7B to start a large flower bud on a longer strand. Complete the large bud as before following step 4 from fig 8 to the end of step 8.

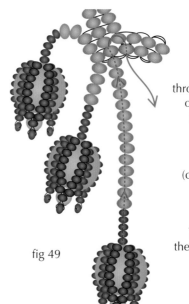

Pass the needle up through the 5B and 14A of the strand. Pass up the bottom 1A of the foundation.

Pass down the next (central) A bead of the foundation (fig 49).

This A bead supports the crystal tassel strand.

fig 49

The Necklace is Made in Four Stages

The first stage establishes the foundation rows across the bottom of the central V. The flower buds up one side of the V are made as the first stem is developed.

Two flowers are added to the bottom of the foundation row along with the crystal tassel strands in stage two.

The third stage adds the opposite stem and flower buds to complete the V.

Finally the side straps are added to the required length.

36 The Crystal Tassel Strand - A long central strand supports two side strands to create a three-stranded tassel.

Thread on 33A, 1F, 1A, 2B, 1A, 1H, 1A, 1F, 1J, 1A, 1G, 1F and 1B. Leaving aside the last B bead to anchor the strand pass the needle back up the previous F and the following beads to emerge above the first F bead of the sequence (fig 50).

Pass the needle through the following 19A. This is the correct position to make the first side strand.

fig 50

37 Thread on 15A, 1F, 1A, 2B, 1A, 1H, 1A, 1F, 1J, 1A, 1G, 1F and 1B.

As before leave aside the last B bead to anchor the strand and pass back up through the beads just added, including the 15A, to emerge at the junction with the first strand (fig 51).

Pass up through the following 5A of the first strand (fig 52).

This is the correct position to start the second side strand.

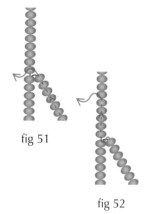

fig 51

fig 52

Thread on 17A, 1F, 1A, 2B, 1A, 1H, 1A, 1F, 1J, 1A, 1G, 1F and 1B.

Make the anchor as before passing the needle through the 17A to the junction and up through the top 9A of the first strand (see fig 53).

Pass up through the A bead of the foundation and down through the next A along (fig 53).

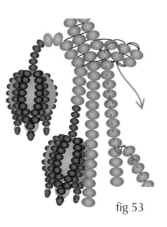

fig 53

38 Thread on 12A, 5B, 1C and 7B to start a large flower bud. Complete the bud as before, passing the needle back up the strand, the A bead on the foundation and down through the next (last) A along the bottom row. This is the correct position to begin the first bud on this edge of the design.

Repeat from step 4 to step 20 to make a mirror image set of three large and three small flower buds (see fig 54).

Referring to step 21 extend the main stem by 6A instead of 8A and add the final small flower, following step 16, to this side of the centrepiece.

Referring to fig 54 pass the needle down the stem beads to emerge from the bottom of the second step along.

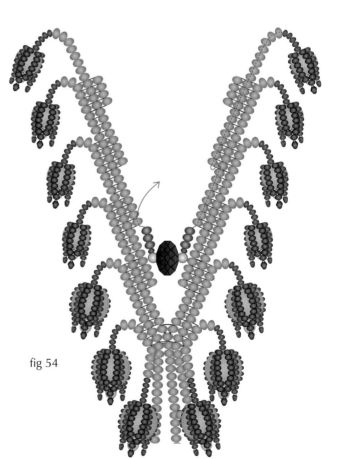

fig 54

39 Thread on 3A, 1B, 1E, 1J, 1E, 1B and 3A. Pass the needle up through the corresponding stem on the other side of the centrepiece (fig 54).
Pass through the following 5A up the stem and finish off this thread end neatly and securely.

40 Before you finish the remaining thread ends you need to make one more stitch. The two longest bud stems at the centre front need to be caught together with a simple square stitch.

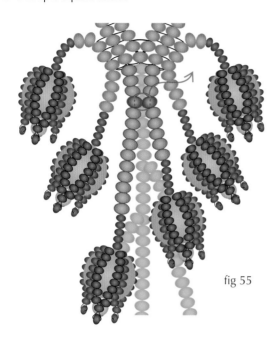

fig 55

Using the closest thread end, or a new thread if the needle will not pass through the beads of the foundation rows again, square stitch the fourth A bead from the top of the 16A strand to the corresponding A bead on the 12A strand (fig 55). This pulls the centre of the V in a little tighter and pushes the plain A beads at the top of the crystal tassel strands to the back of the design.

Remove any remaining keeper beads and finish off all thread ends, neatly and securely, without blocking any bead holes on the stems of the top two small buds on each side of the design.

41 The Side Straps - These attach to the exposed 4A stem sections just below the last buds worked on each side of the V centrepiece.

Prepare the needle with 1.5m of single thread and thread on 1E, 1A, 1G, 2A, 1B and 1E. Pass the needle down the exposed 4A stem section on the left of the V.

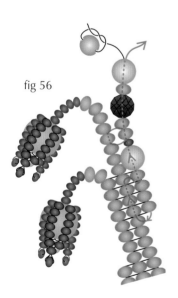

fig 56

Referring to fig 56 pass the needle up through 3A of the adjacent column, the top A of the 4A section and the following 1E, 1B and 1A.

Square stitch this A bead to the fourth A of the stem supporting the top bud. Pass through the following strand beads to emerge at the keeper bead (fig 56).

Thread on 1J, 1A, 1C, 1E, 1G, 1A, 1F, 1A, 1D, 1F, 1A, 1G, 1F and 1A. This completes the connecting sequence.

42 Thread on 10B, 1A, 1F, 1G, 1F, 1A, 20B, 1A, 1F, 1G, 1F, 1A, 30B, 1A, 1F, 1G, 1F, 1A, 40B, 1A, 1F, 1G, 1F and 1A followed by sufficient B beads to make this side of the necklace to your required length - make a note of this B bead count.

The Bead Tag - Thread on 1A, 1F, 1G, 1A, 1B, 1F, 1J, 1F, 1A and 3B. Leaving aside the last 3B to anchor the strand pass the needle back through the beads just added to emerge from the first A bead of the tag (fig 57).

fig 57

43 Thread on the noted number of B beads from step 42 and pass through the first 1A, 1F, 1G, 1F and 1A sequence back along the strand (fig 58).

fig 58

Thread on 40B and pass back through the next 1A, 1F, 1G, 1F and 1A sequence.

Thread on 30B and pass back through the next 1A, 1F, 1G, 1F and 1A sequence.

Thread on 20B and pass back through the next 1A, 1F, 1G, 1F and 1A sequence.

Thread on 10B. Pass back through the last six beads of the connection sequence of step 41 to emerge from the D bead (fig 59).

fig 59

44 Thread on 5B and pass through the D bead again (fig 60). Repeat five times to make six straps of 5B in total.

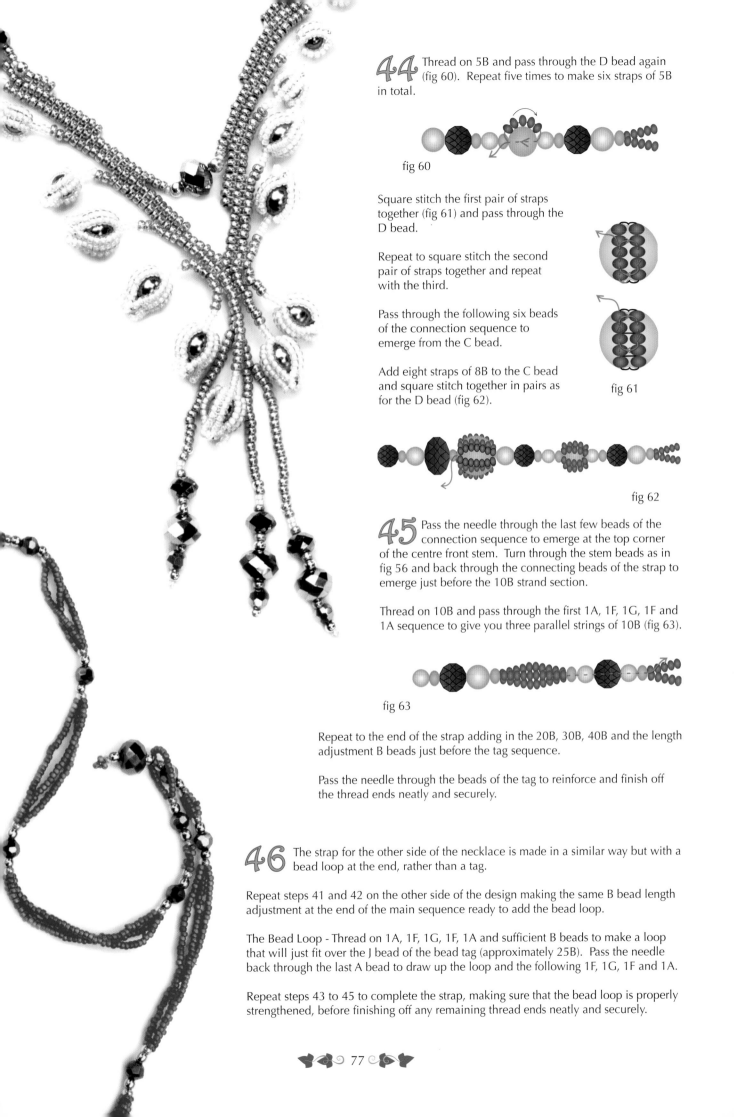

fig 60

Square stitch the first pair of straps together (fig 61) and pass through the D bead.

Repeat to square stitch the second pair of straps together and repeat with the third.

Pass through the following six beads of the connection sequence to emerge from the C bead.

Add eight straps of 8B to the C bead and square stitch together in pairs as for the D bead (fig 62).

fig 61

fig 62

45 Pass the needle through the last few beads of the connection sequence to emerge at the top corner of the centre front stem. Turn through the stem beads as in fig 56 and back through the connecting beads of the strap to emerge just before the 10B strand section.

Thread on 10B and pass through the first 1A, 1F, 1G, 1F and 1A sequence to give you three parallel strings of 10B (fig 63).

fig 63

Repeat to the end of the strap adding in the 20B, 30B, 40B and the length adjustment B beads just before the tag sequence.

Pass the needle through the beads of the tag to reinforce and finish off the thread ends neatly and securely.

46 The strap for the other side of the necklace is made in a similar way but with a bead loop at the end, rather than a tag.

Repeat steps 41 and 42 on the other side of the design making the same B bead length adjustment at the end of the main sequence ready to add the bead loop.

The Bead Loop - Thread on 1A, 1F, 1G, 1F, 1A and sufficient B beads to make a loop that will just fit over the J bead of the bead tag (approximately 25B). Pass the needle back through the last A bead to draw up the loop and the following 1F, 1G, 1F and 1A.

Repeat steps 43 to 45 to complete the strap, making sure that the bead loop is properly strengthened, before finishing off any remaining thread ends neatly and securely.

Papillon
Necklace

necklace measures 44cm

Fluttering

fantasy butterflies and subtle moths are to be found here.

A versatile butterfly motif is imagined in many guises - jewel box bright, pastel perfection, twilight whispers and elegantly tasselled glamour.

To Make the Necklace

3g of size 10/0 silver lined magenta seed beads A
3g of size 10/0 silver lined orange seed beads B
3g of size 10/0 silver lined lime green seed beads C
4g of size 10/0 silver lined sapphire blue seed beads D
8g of size 10/0 silver lined teal seed beads E
2g of size 10/0 frost metallic gold seed beads F
3g of size 8/0 frost metallic gold seed beads G
2g of size 6/0 frost metallic gold seed beads H
Eleven 6mm frost metallic gold round beads K
Eleven 3x1.5mm red crystal rondelle beads L
Six 3x1.5mm teal crystal rondelle beads M
Two 3x1.5mm emerald crystal rondelle beads N
Twelve 4x6mm red crystal rondelle beads P
Seven 4x6mm teal crystal rondelle beads Q
Three 4x6mm emerald crystal rondelle beads R
One 6x8mm red crystal rondelle bead S
One 6x8mm teal crystal rondelle bead T
One 6x8mm emerald crystal rondelle bead U
Black size D beading thread

Tools

A size 10 beading needle
A pair of scissors to trim the threads

The Necklace is Made in Three Stages

The nine butterflies are made as separate motifs.
The butterflies are arranged in order and stitched together.
The side straps are added to finish the necklace.

1 The Butterflies - Prepare the needle with 1.2m of single thread and tie a keeper bead 15cm from the end. Thread on 1K for the body of the butterfly.

Pass the needle through the K bead to make a thread strap on the side of the bead (fig 1). Repeat to make a second strap on the other side of the K bead (fig 2).
Repeat to make a double strap of thread on each side.

These straps will support the first row of seed beads.

2 Thread on 1F and 1A. Pass the needle under both thread straps on one side of the K bead and back up through the A bead (fig 3).

Pull the thread through gently so the two seed beads sit side-by-side with their holes close to parallel (fig 4).

3 Thread on 1A. Pass the needle under the thread straps adjacent to the previous A bead and back up through the new A (fig 5). Pull the bead into place so it sits on the thread strap. This is brick stitch.

Repeat step 3 twice to add two more single A stitches.

4 Thread on 1F. Pass through the K bead and the F bead at the far end (fig 6).

Add four single A bead brick stitches to the thread straps on the other side of the K bead (fig 7).

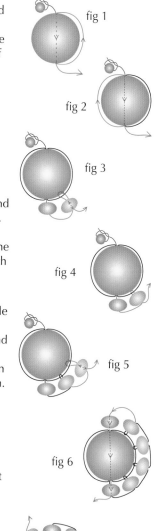

fig 1

fig 2

fig 3

fig 4

fig 5

fig 6

fig 7

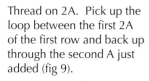

fig 8

5 Pass the needle down though the F bead at this end of the K bead, the K bead and the first A bead added in step 2 to emerge as fig 8 pointing away from the K bead.

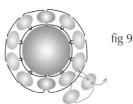

fig 9

Thread on 2A. Pick up the loop between the first 2A of the first row and back up through the second A just added (fig 9).

Pull the thread through so the new beads sit on top of the previous row with the first A bead of this row over-hanging the first A bead of the previous row (fig 10).

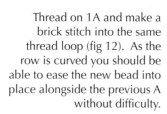

fig 10

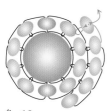

fig 11

6 Thread on 1A and make a brick stitch picking up the next thread loop (fig 11). You now have to make an increase stitch.

Thread on 1A and make a brick stitch into the same thread loop (fig 12). As the row is curved you should be able to ease the new bead into place alongside the previous A without difficulty.

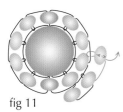

fig 12

Thread on 1A and make a brick stitch picking up the next loop along (fig 13). This is the last bead of the row.

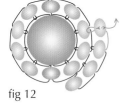

fig 13

7 Thread on 1A and 1B. Pick up the last thread loop of the previous row and pass back up the B bead (fig 14).

Add 1A stitch, an increase A stitch and 1A as step 6.

Add 1B stitch.

Referring to fig 15 thread on 1A and pass down the first bead of the previous row to complete this row.

Pass the needle up the parallel A bead and the last B of the of the row just completed (fig 15).

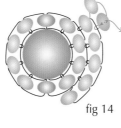

fig 14

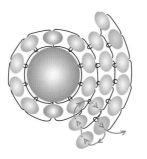

fig 15

8 Thread on 1L and 4B. Pass the needle through the first B of the 4B in the same direction to bring these seed beads into a circle (fig 16).

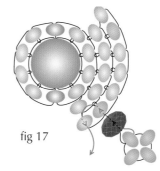

fig 16

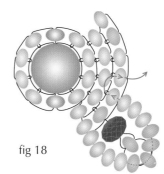

fig 17

Pass back down the L bead and the B bead beneath it. Pass up through the A bead at the end of the previous row (fig 17).

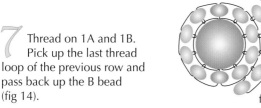

fig 18

9 Thread on 4A. Pass the needle through the 3B beads around the top of the circle of 4B and thread on 1B and 3A.

Pass the needle down the brick-stitched A bead to the other side of the L bead and up through the next A bead along the previous row (fig 18).

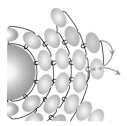

fig 19

10 Thread on 1A and 1B. Pick up the second loop (between the A and B beads) and pass back up the B bead just added (fig 19). This stretches the stitch across the gap but the A bead will tend to tip.

To correct the 'tip' pass the needle down the new A bead, pick up the thread loop below it (between two A beads) and pass back up the new A bead (fig 20).

Repeat this stitch on the B bead to reposition the needle (fig 21).

fig 20

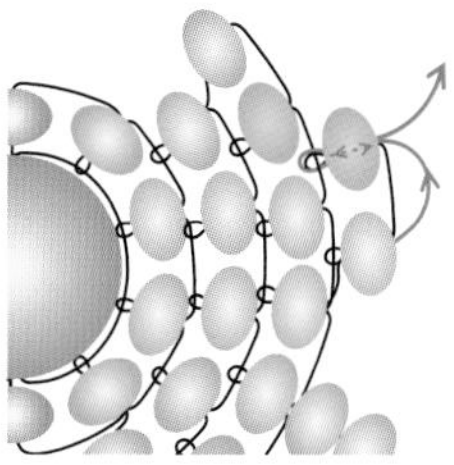

fig 21

11 Make 1B bead stitch picking up the next loop along. Thread on 1A and pass the needle down the first A of the previous row to complete this row.

Pass the needle up the parallel B bead and the B bead just added (fig 22).

fig 22

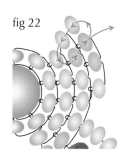

fig 23

fig 24

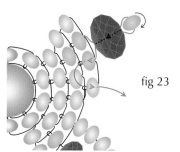

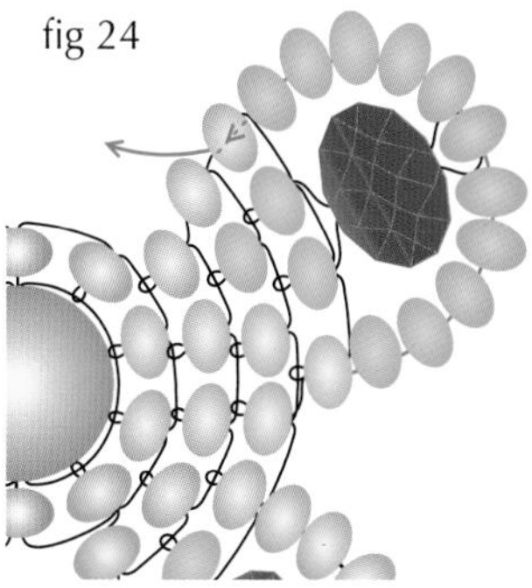

12 Thread on 1P and 1B. Pass the needle back down the P bead and through the first B added in step 10. Pass up through the parallel A bead (fig 23).

Thread on 5B. Pass through the single B at the top of the P bead and thread on 5B. Pass down the A bead on the other side of the P bead (fig 24).

fig 25

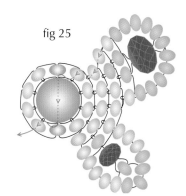

13 Pass down the following 2A and the A bead closest to the hole in the K bead. Pass down the K bead and through the A bead closest to the hole on the opposite side of the K (fig 25).

This is the correct position to start the wings on this side of the K bead.

Repeat from fig 9 in step 5 to step 12 to make the wings on this side of the body.

fig 26

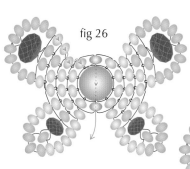

14 Pass down the following 2A and the A bead closest to the hole in the K bead. Pass down the K bead and through the F bead at the bottom (fig 26).

Thread on 3G and 1F. Pass the needle back up the 3G, the F below the K bead, the K and the following 1F. Thread on 1H for the head and pass back down the F bead only (fig 27).

fig 27

fig 28

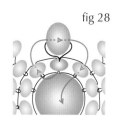

Pass up the adjacent A bead, through the H bead and down the A bead on the other side of the F. Use this thread pass to stabilise the H bead so the hole runs at 90º to the body beads (fig 28). The beading for the butterfly is complete.

Remove the needle, leave the thread ends attached and set aside.

Following the same method make eight more butterflies -

Make one identical butterfly motif with A on the inner part of the wings, B on the outer part using L and P crystals. Make one butterfly with the A and B beads reversed using the L and P crystals.

Make two butterflies with C for the inner part of the wings, A for the outer part, using M and Q crystals. Make one butterfly with the C and A beads reversed using the M and Q crystals.

Make two butterflies with D for the inner part of the wings, E for the outer part, using L and P crystals.

Make one butterfly with E for the inner part of the wings, D for the outer part, using N and R crystals.

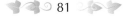

15 Assembling the Butterfly Centrepiece -
Fig 29 shows the layout for the butterflies.
The butterflies are linked together where they
touch - the ideal positions for the joins are
highlighted but you may find that your links vary
by a bead to one side or the other.

fig 29

Lay your butterflies out as shown. The seven motifs across the top line should contact each other at two locations and be symmetrical. You will need to stitch two beads from each motif together at each of these locations. Matching up two beads in two locations between each pair of motifs gives the top line of the design stability and prevents any distortion when worn.

The two butterflies that hang below the central motif are linked by a single bead to a single bead (apart from the larger H bead) to give more flexibility and 'lightness' to this section.

16 Start with the links along the top line working out from the centre-front to either side.

Attach the needle to the longest thread end on the central butterfly and pass it through the beads of the wings to emerge at the first two-bead link on the right-hand wings.

Pass through the two beads on the wing of the adjacent butterfly and back through the two on the central butterfly wing to make a square stitch (fig 30).

fig 31

Repeat the stitch to make the link firm. Pass the needle through to the next link location and repeat.

Pass the needle through the beads around the perimeter of the wings of the central butterfly to both make the wings more firm, and relocate the needle to the other side of the motif, ready to make the links on the left.

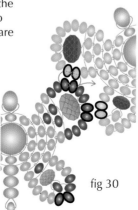

fig 30

17 Move onto the other links along the top line - in each case use the longest thread on each motif to make the links and pass the needle around the perimeter beads on each wing to make them more firm.

Do not finish off any thread ends yet.

Make the single bead links to attach the two dangling butterflies at the centre-front in the same manner - note the H head bead link needs to join onto two beads on the centre-front butterfly.

Repeat to add the butterfly motif to the left of the centre-front (fig 31). Leave the thread ends loose and remove the needle.

18 Return to the thread
ends.
One by one attach the needle to
each end, and where thread length
allows, pass through the beads
around the perimeter of each motif
before finishing off neatly and securely.
Do not block the holes in the beads on
the outermost wings at either side of the
centrepiece - you still need to attach the side
straps to these beads.

19 The Side Straps - Prepare the needle with
1.2m of single thread and tie a keeper bead
15cm from the end. Thread on 1K.

Add the thread straps as in step
1 and using D beads only repeat
steps 2, 3 and 4 up to fig 7.

Pass the needle down the adjacent
D bead at this end of the K bead,
the K bead and the D bead at the
far end to complete a frame of
10D around the K bead (fig 32).

fig 32

20 Thread on 1A, 1Q, 1A, 1U and 3D. Pick up
the end butterfly of the centrepiece with A
beads around the edge of the wings. Counting out
along the top edge of the outside wing locate
the tenth and eleventh beads.

Referring to fig 33 pass
through these 2A beads and
thread on 2D. Pass up
through the first 1D of
the 3D beads and the
following 1U, 1A, 1Q,
1A, 1D, 1K and 1D
(fig 33).

fig 33

21 Thread on 1A, 2E, 1P, 1E and 1G.

Mix a small pinch of D beads with the E beads - call this
mixture V. Thread on sufficient V to make a strand of your
preferred length.

22 Thread on 1G, 1S,
1D and 3C.
Leaving aside the 3C beads to anchor
the strand pass the needle back through
the last D bead and the following S and G
beads (fig 34).

fig 34

Thread on the same length of V beads as before to create
the second strand of the side strap.

23 Pass the needle down through the 1G, 1E, 1P, 2E,
1A and the following beads of the sequence to the
butterfly motif, through the 2A on the butterfly wing and
back up through the strap beads to emerge at the base of
the first V strand.

Pass up through these V beads, the beads of the tag at the
end and back down the second V strand to strengthen the
work. Pass through to emerge at the keeper bead. Finish off
both thread ends neatly and securely.

24 Repeat steps 19 to 21. This side of the necklace
requires the bead loop to complete the clasp.

Thread on 1G and 1L followed by sufficient V beads to
make a loop that will just fit over the S bead of the tag
(approximately19V). Pass the needle back through the L
and G beads to draw up the loop (fig 35).

fig 35

Thread on the same length of V beads as before to create
the second string of the side strap.

Repeat step 23 reinforcing the V beads of the bead loop
like those of the tag.

Lysandra Necklace

A simple stringing of a single Papillon motif makes the sweetest summer necklace.

You Will Need

To Make the Necklace

6g of size 10/0 alabaster pale tanzanite seed beads A
9g of size 10/0 alabaster periwinkle seed beads B
0.5g of size 10/0 frost metallic silver seed beads F
2g of size 8/0 frost metallic silver seed beads G
One size 6/0 frost metallic silver seed bead H
Two 6mm frost metallic silver round beads K
Two 3x1.5mm pink crystal rondelle beads L
Two 4x6mm pink crystal rondelle beads P
Five 4x6mm clear AB crystal rondelle beads Q
Baby pink size D beading thread

necklace measures 44cm

25 Follow steps 1 to 14 to make a butterfly motif.

Pass the needle down through the K body bead and the 1F, 3G and 1F of the tail (fig 36).

fig 36

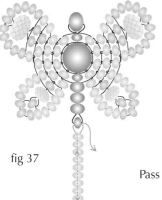

fig 37

26 Thread on 10A, 1B, 1Q, 1B and 1A. Leaving aside the last A bead to anchor the strand pass the needle back up the 1B, 1Q, 1B and 10A.

Pass the needle through the F bead at the base of the tail (fig 37).

Finish off this thread end neatly and securely.

27 Prepare the needle with 1m of single thread and tie a keeper bead 15cm from the end. Counting along the top edge of the top wing pass the needle through the first 5B beads to emerge as shown in fig 38.

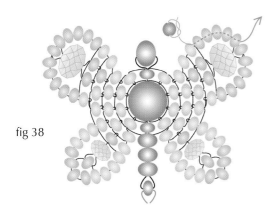

fig 38

Thread on 1Q, 1F, 1A, 1G, 3A, 1B, 1G, 13B, 1A, 1G, 1A, 15B, 1A, 1G, 1A, 17B, 1A, 1G, 1A, 19B, 1A, 1G, 1A, 21B, 1A, 1G, 1A, 23B, 1A, 1G, 1A followed by sufficient B beads to make the string up to the required length for this side of the necklace.

28 Thread on 1A, 1G, 1A, 1K, 1A, 1F and 3B. Leave aside the last 3B to anchor the strand and pass the needle back through the last F bead and the previous five beads to make the bead tag half of the clasp (fig 39).

fig 39

29 Pass back through the following beads to emerge from the second G bead of the string sequence.

Thread on 1B, 5A, 2B, 5A, 3B and 6A. Referring to fig 40 pass the needle through the third B bead along the top edge of the lower wing on this side of the motif.

30 Thread on 5A, 1B, 1Q, 1B and 1A. Leave aside the last A bead to anchor the strand and pass back up the other eight beads just added.

Pass through the B bead on the motif in the opposite direction (fig 40).

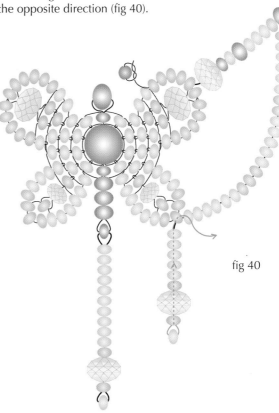

fig 40

Pass through the following 22 beads added in step 29 and the beads of the main string up to the bead tag added in step 28. Pass the needle through the tag beads and back down the main string - this time pass the needle through to the top edge of the top wing to emerge at the keeper bead added in step 27.

Before you finish the ends pass the needle through the beads around the edge of both wings on this side of the body to make it more firm. Repeat if the needle will pass through the holes again.
Finish off the thread ends neatly and securely.

31 Repeat step 27 on the other side of the motif. You need to add a bead loop to the end of this string.

Thread on 1A, 1F and 1A followed by sufficient B beads to make a loop that will just fit over the K bead of the bead tag (approximately 17B). Pass the needle back through the 1A, 1F and 1A beads to draw up the loop.

Repeat from step 29 to complete this side of the design before finishing off any remaining thread ends neatly and securely.

Fritillary Necklace

A flutter of subtly-shaded butterflies to nestle around the neck.
This arrangement of seventeen motifs measures 44cm but you can make
it longer with a few more motifs, if you wish.

This necklace uses five colours of seed
beads for the wings and four colours of
crystal. These are mixed, matched and
reversed to make a fantasy assortment
of toning wings - no two butterflies
are the same.

The frosted metallic silver chosen for the
body beads brings harmony to the design.

Draw a simple line (to scale) of the size
of necklace you want to make and lay the
butterflies down onto the line.
Twist and turn them until they make a
pleasing arrangement and stitch them
together as in step 16.

necklace measures 44cm

Nocturne Sautoir

Elegant tassel strands, butterfly wings and a moonlight palette brings a touch of Art Nouveau to this design.

Following the Papillon instructions work up to fig 26 to make three sets of wings.

Make the tassel separately with seven strands of seed beads, bugles and crystals dangling from a 12mm fire polished faceted bead. The needle is turned for each new tassel strand through a size 8/0 seed bead immediately above the large facet.

Link the top of the tassel to the centre butterfly creating the lower part of the body and adding the head bead at the same time (fig 41).
This completes the pendant.

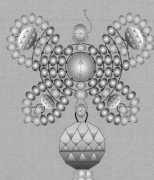

fig 41

Add the main string with a double thickness of thread.

Note how the two butterflies on either side of the pendant are completed, with the head and body beads as part of the main stringing sequence.

necklace measures 74cm

Honeycomb
Necklace & Bracelet

necklace measures 43cm
bracelet measures 18cm

Humming

honeycombs of perfect symmetry are a marvel to behold.

These simple-to-make hexagons can be assembled into many combinations - here are a necklace, a bracelet and a very cute bee-house box.

You Will Need

To Make the Necklace

12g of DB2184 semi-frost silver lined bramble Delica beads A
12g of DB2177 semi-frost silver lined mica Delica beads B
1g of DB2102 opaque banana Delica beads C
3g of size 15/0 frost opaque white seed beads D
Two 6x8mm opal white crystal rondelles E
0.4g of size 15/0 lustre yellow seed beads F
0.4g of size 15/0 frost transparent brown seed beads G
0.8g of size 15/0 silver lined crystal seed beads H
Two 4mm black fire polished faceted beads K
Three size 6/0 black seed beads L
0.4g of size 11/0 frost black seed beads M
3g of silver lined dark grey Twin beads P
3g of silver lined pale apricot Twin beads Q
Grey, white and black
size D beading thread

To Make the Bracelet

8g of DB2184 semi-frost silver lined bramble Delica beads A
8g of DB2177 semi-frost silver lined mica Delica beads B
0.2g of DB2102 opaque banana Delica beads C
1g of size 15/0 frost opaque white seed beads D
0.4g of size 15/0 lustre yellow seed beads F
0.4g of size 15/0 frost transparent brown seed beads G
0.8g of size 15/0 silver lined crystal seed beads H
Two 4mm black fire polished faceted beads K
Two size 6/0 black seed beads L
0.4g of size 11/0 frost black seed beads M
2g of silver lined dark grey Twin beads P
2g of silver lined pale apricot Twin beads Q
Grey, white and black
size D beading thread

Tools
A size 13 beading needle
A pair of scissors to trim the threads

The Necklace is Made in Five Stages

The honeycomb hexagons are made in peyote stitch.
The daisy flowers are made.
The bees are made.
The hexagons are linked together to make the honeycomb with the daisies and bees stitched into place to complete the centrepiece.
The side straps are added to complete the design.

1 The Hexagons - Each hexagon is made from six, linked peyote-stitched tubes. Prepare the needle with 1m of single grey thread and tie a keeper bead 15cm from the end.

Thread on 7A for the first row.

Thread on 1A and pass back through the sixth A of the first row (fig 1).

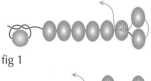

fig 1

Thread on 1A and pass back through the fourth A of the first row (fig 2).

Thread on 1A and pass back through the second A of the first row. Thread on 1A and push it up to sit alongside the first A of the first row with the holes parallel (fig 3).

fig 2

fig 3

You have made a series of keys and keyholes. In the next row the needle passes through the key beads to add beads into the keyholes. This in turn creates a new row of keys and key-holes. This is peyote stitch.

Extra Info....

The first row of each peyote stitch tube has an odd number of beads. An odd number of beads causes a slight problem on alternate rows as the needle finishes in the wrong position, to immediately turn and start the next row.

It's easily solved with a stitch though the beads of the previous row, very much like a three-point turn in a car, allowing the needle to emerge, pointing in the correct direction, ready for the new row - see step 4.

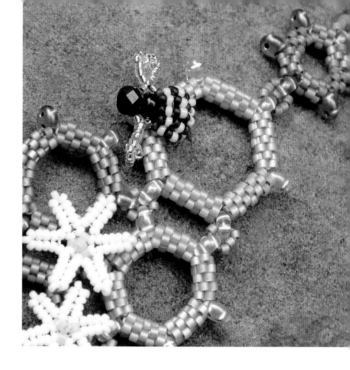

2 Turn the Corner - Pass the needle through the first bead of the previous row to point back along that row (fig 4). Make sure that the last bead of the previous row is sitting neatly in place (as fig 4).

fig 4

Thread on 1A and pass through the next key bead (fig 5).

fig 5

Repeat to add 1A into the next keyhole. Repeat to add 1A in the last keyhole (fig 6).

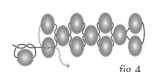

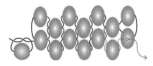

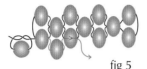

fig 6

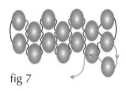

fig 7

3 Thread on 1A and pass back through the first key bead of previous row (fig 7).

Repeat to the end of the row - the last bead of the row should nestle into the last gap (fig 8). You now need to turn the needle for the new row.

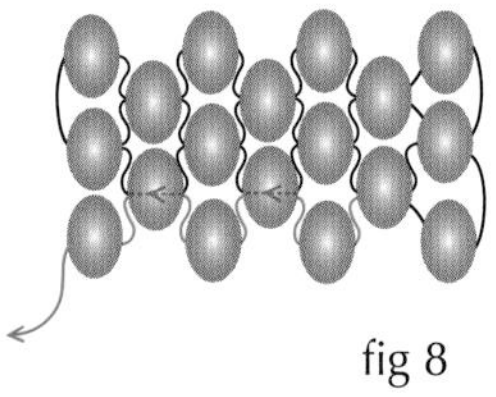

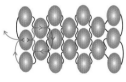

fig 8

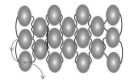

fig 9

4 Pass back through the adjacent end bead and the diagonally-positioned bead next to it. Turn the needle and pass through the parallel bead and the same end bead (fig 9).

Pass back through the last bead of the row just completed (fig 10).

fig 10

The last bead added is now secure and the needle has been turned to point in the correct direction for the first bead of the new row.

5 Add 1A in the three keyholes along this row.

Repeat steps 3 and 4 to add one more row and turn the corner ready for the last row of Peyote stitch.

Add 1A in each of the three keyholes along this row (fig 11).

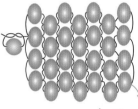

fig 11

6 Roll the beadwork into a tube so the key beads of row one fit into the keyholes of the last row worked.

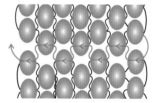

fig 12

Zip the two edges together (fig 12).

At the far end of the tube turn the needle and bring it back along the seam to make it firm and secure.

This completes the first tube of the hexagon.

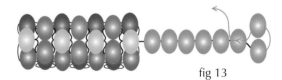

fig 13

7 Thread on 7A and push down to the end of the tube just completed. This is the first row of the next tube.

Thread on 1A and pass back through the sixth A of the first row (fig 13). Make sure that this stitch pushes the first row beads up snugly to the end of the previous tube.

Work the remainder of this tube as for the first tube completing it with the zipped seam as in step 6.

8 Examine fig 14 - this shows the correct position for the needle to be in to start the next tube.

fig 14

The needle is in line with the connection from the previous tube. At present your needle will be one or two beads out of place at the end of the tube just completed.

Pass the needle up and down through the beads at the end of the tube, if necessary turning in the work as in step 4, to emerge as fig 14 ready to start the next tube.

Repeat steps 7 and 8 until you have six tubes in a linked row. Finish with the needle as in fig 14, in line with all the previous links.

You now need to link the sixth tube to the first tube.

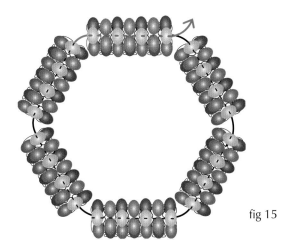

fig 15

9 Referring to fig 15 pick up the first tube and pass the needle through the 4A beads in line with the link between the first and second tubes.

Pull the sixth tube up snugly to make the hexagon - the links should pull to the inner edge of the hexagon forming six V-shaped gaps around the outer edge (fig 16).

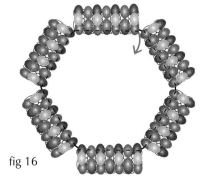

fig 16

The hexagon needs to be strengthened along the inner edge.

Pass the needle through the 4A beads in line with the next link (between tubes two and three).

Repeat until the needle has made a complete circuit around the inner edge of the hexagon to reinforce the links. Repeat once more to reinforce the link between the sixth tube and the first tube.

10 Reposition the needle to emerge from the opposite A bead at the end of the current tube (fig 17).

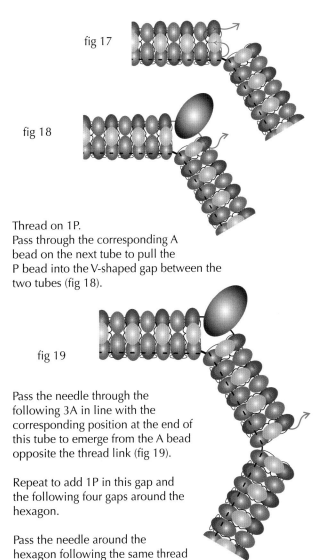

fig 17

fig 18

Thread on 1P.
Pass through the corresponding A bead on the next tube to pull the P bead into the V-shaped gap between the two tubes (fig 18).

fig 19

Pass the needle through the following 3A in line with the corresponding position at the end of this tube to emerge from the A bead opposite the thread link (fig 19).

Repeat to add 1P in this gap and the following four gaps around the hexagon.

Pass the needle around the hexagon following the same thread path again to make the work firm.

Remove the needle and the keeper bead. Attach the needle to the short tail and finish off this end neatly and securely without blocking the holes in the P beads. The long thread end will be used again when the design is assembled.

Repeat from step 1 to make two hexagons in B and Q beads, with sides seven beads long.

Repeat the technique to make three hexagons in A and P beads, using just five beads for row one.

Repeat the technique to make two hexagons in B and Q beads, using just five beads for row one.

Repeat the technique to make one hexagon in A and P beads, using just three beads for row one.

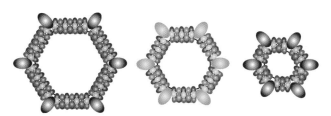

Hexagons with Sides Seven, Five and Three Beads Long

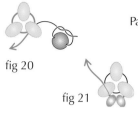

11 The Daisies - The daisies are made in herringbone stitch. The small daisies are made first.

Prepare the needle with 80cm of single white thread and tie a keeper bead 15cm from the end. Thread on 3C.

Pass the needle through the first C again to make a small triangle of beads (fig 20). Pass the needle through the 3C again to make the triangle firm.

fig 20

fig 21

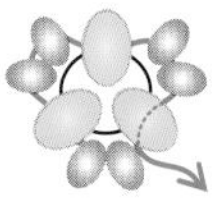

fig 22

fig 23

12 Thread on 2D and pass through the next C (fig 21).

Repeat twice (fig 22).

Pass through the first 1D to reposition the needle for the next row (fig 23).

Thread on 2D. Pass through the next D bead and the following 1C and 1D to pull the new 2D into a V-shape between the first 2D of the previous row (fig 24).

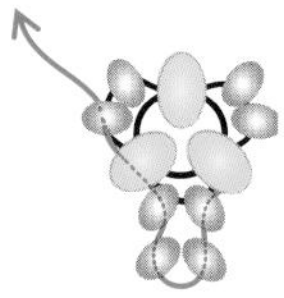

fig 24

Repeat twice (fig 25). You now have three columns of C beads, each 2C wide.

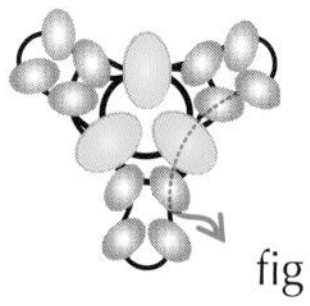

fig 25

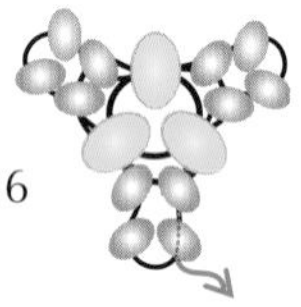

fig 26

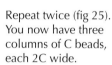

Pass the needle through the first D of the row just completed to reposition the needle for the new row (fig 26).

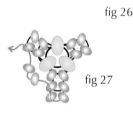

fig 27

fig 28

13 Thread on 2D. Pass the needle down through the second D at the top of this column and thread on 2D. Pass the needle up through the adjacent top D of the next column (fig 27).

Repeat once.

fig 29

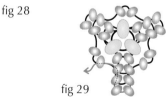

fig 30

Thread on 2D. Pass the needle down through the second D at the top of this column and thread on 2D. Pass the needle up through the top 2D of the next column (fig 28) - this completes the row and repositions the needle for the next row.

14 Thread on 2D. Pass the needle down through the second D at the top of this column and the following 1D. Pass the needle up through the next D (fig 29).

Thread on 2D. Pass the needle down through the next D bead and up through the top 2D of the adjacent column (fig 30). Note that you are creating another herringbone column.

Repeat step 14 once.

Repeat again passing the needle up through the top 3D of the first column to finish the row and reposition the needle for the next row (fig 31). You now have six columns - three of which are 4D high and three are 2D high.

15 Thread on 3D. Pass the needle down the second D at the top of the column and the following 2D to make a petal point. Pass up through the 2D of the next column (fig 32).

This column needs to be extended by one stitch before you add the petal point.

fig 31

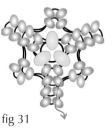

fig 32

16 Thread on 2D. Pass down the following 2D, back up the adjacent 2D and the first of the 2D just added (fig 33).

Thread on 3D. Pass down the following 3D and up the adjacent 3D of the next column (fig 34).

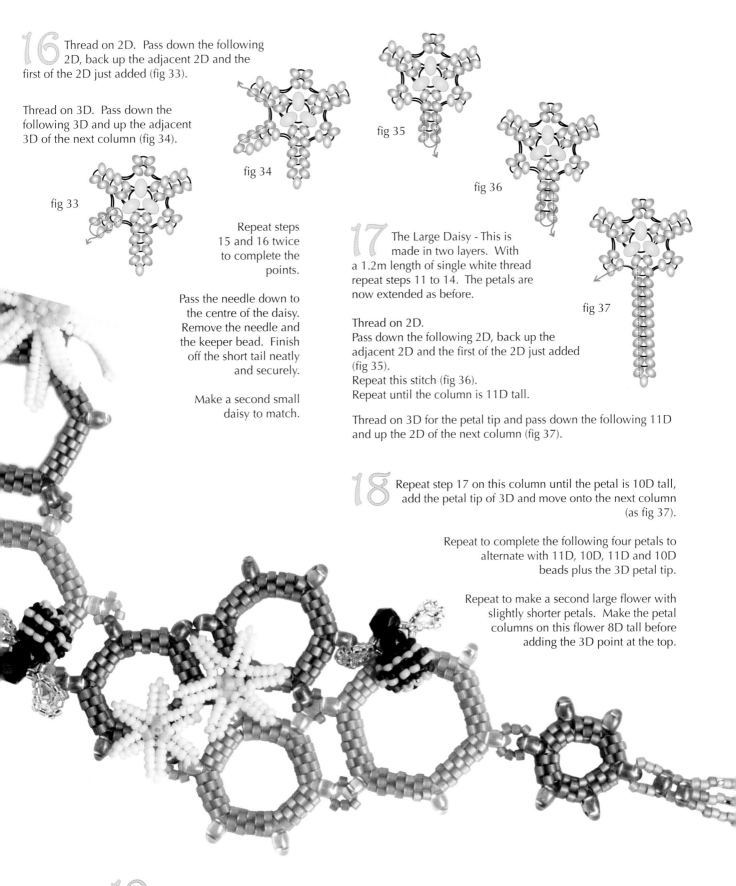

fig 33

fig 34

fig 35

fig 36

fig 37

Repeat steps 15 and 16 twice to complete the points.

Pass the needle down to the centre of the daisy. Remove the needle and the keeper bead. Finish off the short tail neatly and securely.

Make a second small daisy to match.

17 The Large Daisy - This is made in two layers. With a 1.2m length of single white thread repeat steps 11 to 14. The petals are now extended as before.

Thread on 2D.
Pass down the following 2D, back up the adjacent 2D and the first of the 2D just added (fig 35).
Repeat this stitch (fig 36).
Repeat until the column is 11D tall.

Thread on 3D for the petal tip and pass down the following 11D and up the 2D of the next column (fig 37).

18 Repeat step 17 on this column until the petal is 10D tall, add the petal tip of 3D and move onto the next column (as fig 37).

Repeat to complete the following four petals to alternate with 11D, 10D, 11D and 10D beads plus the 3D petal tip.

Repeat to make a second large flower with slightly shorter petals. Make the petal columns on this flower 8D tall before adding the 3D point at the top.

19 Remove the keeper beads on both flowers. Attach the needle to the longest thread on the larger flower. Position the slightly smaller flower on top of the large one with the petals arranged so they fall in-between the longer petals and make two or three stitches to secure the two centres together.

Pass the needle to the front of the small flower through the central hole. Thread on 1C and pass back through the central hole to pull the bead up tight. Pass the needle to the front of the flower stack through an adjacent gap between the C beads and repeat. Repeat this stitch to build up a compact, slightly domed centre of neatly placed, but randomly orientated, C beads - you will need up to 20C in total.

Finish off all but the longest remaining thread neatly and securely.

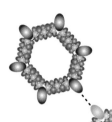

20 The Bees - Referring to the bee instructions on pages 59 and 60 in the Sunflower Necklace chapter, and using black thread make two bees. Finish off the shorter thread end on each bee leaving the longer ends to attach them to the centrepiece.

21 Linking the Hexagons - Arrange the hexagons as shown in fig 38.

You may find that each hexagon has a definite 'right side' and 'wrong side' as the P and Q beads tend to nestle to one face or the other of each unit. Make sure each hexagon is showing the slightly domed face to the front.

fig 38

Extra Info....
If you want to wear your necklace a little longer you may want to rearrange the hexagons before you stitch them together. A slightly narrower, more vertical combination will hang more satisfactorily than the wider design shown in fig 38.

The hexagons are linked together where the P and Q beads touch. Each join will use three or four A and B beads to hold the P and Q beads in the correct orientation. In each join the bead count will need to total up to six. You can use either A or B beads to make the joins - you may prefer to vary them - for simplicity the instructions will refer to A. Use the longest thread end closest to each join - don't finish any ends until step 24.

Start at position X on fig 38. Attach the needle to the closest thread end to this location and pass through the work to emerge at the base of the P or Q bead. Pass through the inner hole of the P or Q and in the opposite direction through the outer hole.

22 Position Y is slightly different as there are just two P and Q beads to link. If necessary, attach the needle to the closest thread end and pass through the work to emerge from the outer hole of the closest P or Q. You need to add 1A to the inner part of the join and 3A to the outer part (fig 40).

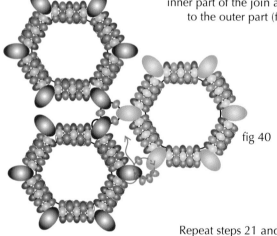

fig 40

Repeat steps 21 and 22 as necessary to link the central seven hexagons where shown in fig 38.

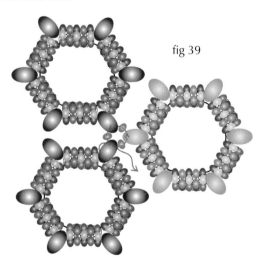

fig 39

23 The last two links, shown by dotted lines on fig 38, stretch out to either side and link two P and Q beads together in a straight line. To increase the flexibility 6A beads are used for these links (fig 41).

Make these two links as shown in fig 41.

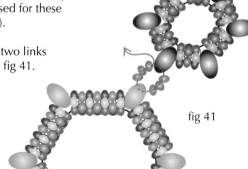

fig 41

Thread on 1A and the next P or Q bead around the join. Repeat until you have linked all of the P and Q beads together and completed the circle (fig 39). Pass the needle around the join twice more to make it firm. Remove the needle if the thread is less than 25cm long.

24 Arrange the bees and the daisies on the honeycomb - the photo on page 88 shows just one possible option. Try to place the motifs on the corners of the hexagons, or on the joins, where it is easier to stitch them down firmly.

Attach the small daisies first, using the attached thread ends, adding 1C into the centre of each as you stitch.
Add the large daisy next and finally the bees.

Finish off all the thread ends neatly and securely.

25 The Side Straps - Put a pinch of A beads aside (approximately 20 beads) for the first part of the straps. Mix the remaining A, B and H beads together - this mix will be used for the main length of the straps and will be called S. The straps attach to the P beads opposite the last links made in step 23.

Prepare the needle with 1.2m of single grey thread and tie a keeper bead 15cm from the end. Locate the P bead on the smallest (3A sided) hexagon opposite the link to the central section of the necklace - this is the P bead you are joining to.

Thread on 1P, 1A, 1P and 3A.

Pass the needle through the outer hole of the P bead on the hexagon and thread on 3A.

Pass the needle through the other hole of the second P and thread on 1A. Pass through the second hole of the first P (fig 42).

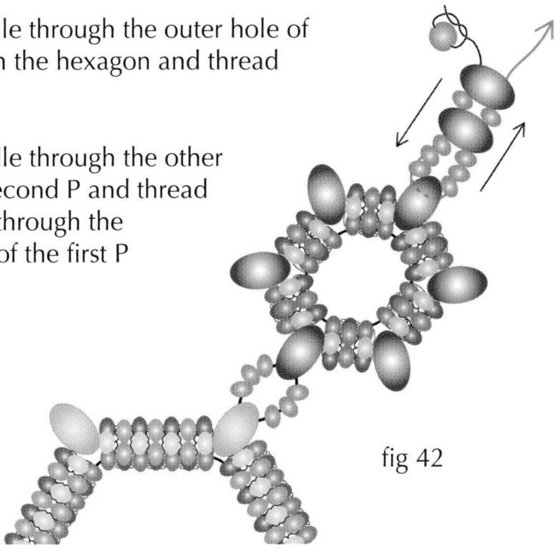

fig 42

Thread on sufficient S beads to make this side of the necklace the desired length.

26 The Bead Loop - Thread on 1C, 1L and 1C. Thread on sufficient assorted size 15 seed beads to make a loop that the E beads (for the other half of the clasp) will just fit through (approximately twenty-six beads). Pass back through the 1C, 1L and 1C to draw up the loop (fig 43).

fig 43

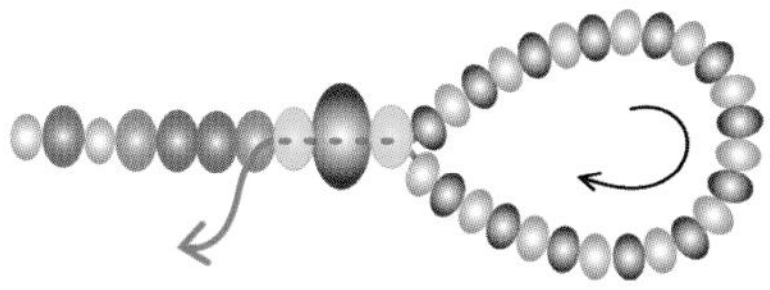

27 Thread on sufficient S beads to reach back to the first P bead of the strap.

Pass through this P bead and the following five beads, through the P on the hexagon and the following six beads to emerge at the start of the first strap (fig 44).

Thread on the same length of S beads as before.

Pass the needle through the beads of the bead loop to strengthen it.

Pass back through the beads of the last strap made to emerge just before the first P bead.

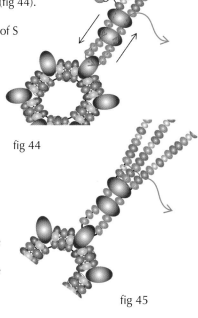

fig 44

28 Square stitch the first 2S of each strap together to neaten the join to the P bead (fig 45) and finish off the thread ends neatly and securely.

fig 45

29 Repeat step 25 on the other side of the necklace front - you'll need to join on to the corresponding P bead on the end hexagon at this side.
The bead tag of the clasp will need to be added to the end of this strap.

The Bead Tag - Thread on 1M, 1E, 1M, 1C, 1M, 1E, 1M, 1S, 1C and 1S. Leaving aside the last three beads threaded to anchor the strand pass back through the last M bead and the following six beads to emerge at the end of the strap (fig 46).

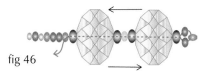

fig 46

Repeat steps 27 and 28 to complete the side strap, adding the second and third strings and reinforcing the bead tag with a second pass of thread.

Finish off all the remaining thread ends neatly and securely.

Honeycomb Bracelet

The Bracelet is Made in Four Stages

The hexagons are made first and linked into a strip.
The bar and loop clasp is added.
The flowers and bees are made.
The motifs are stitched into place along the design.

30 Following the technique in steps 1 to 10 make four hexagons with 5A bead sides and P beads at the corners.

Repeat to make three hexagons of the same size in B and Q beads.

Lay the hexagons in a line, alternating the colours with the P and Q beads touching (fig 47).

fig 47

Referring to the notes in step 21 and the bead positions in step 22 link the P and Q beads together with your choice of either A or B beads.

Check the work for length against your wrist - the clasp will add 15mm when the design is complete. If required make and add one or more hexagons.

Finish off the thread ends neatly and securely.

31 Making the Clasp - The bar is made first. Referring to steps 1 to 6 make a peyote tube starting with a first row of 9B.

Pass the needle through the first 4B of the first row and thread on 2A and 2B.

Referring to fig 48 locate the middle A (or B) bead between the P (or Q) beads at the end of the bracelet. Pass the needle through this bead and thread on 1B.

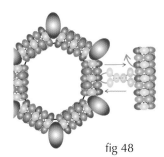

Pass the needle through the central 1B and 1A of the link and thread on 1A. Pass the needle through the sixth B bead of the 9B peyote tube (fig 48).

fig 48

Pass the needle back and forth through these link beads twice more to strengthen it.

Before you finish off the thread ends pass the needle up and down all of the rows of the 9B peyote tube bar to make it stiffer. When the needle will no longer pass through the bead holes finish off the thread ends neatly and securely.

32 The Bead Loop - The strong loop is made from a narrow peyote stitch strap.

Prepare the needle with 1m of single thread and tie a keeper bead 15cm from the end. Thread on 13 repeats of 1A and 1B. These twenty-six beads are the first row of the peyote stitch strap.

33 Using the same technique as for the tubes make a second row in B beads only (see fig 49). Add a third row in A beads only (fig 49).

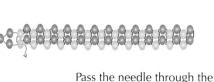

fig 49

Thread on 2A and 2B and referring to fig 50 locate the middle A (or B) bead between the P (or Q) beads at the end of the bracelet. Pass the needle through this bead and thread on 1B.

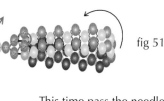

Pass the needle through the central 1B and 1A of the link and thread on 1A. Pass the needle through the other B bead at this end of the peyote stitch strap (fig 50).

fig 50

Turn the needle through the beads at the end of the strip and pass back through the link beads just added. Pass through the bead on the hexagon and back through the link beads.

fig 51

This time pass the needle through the two beads at the other end of the peyote stitch strap to form the loop (fig 51).

Pass the needle back and forth through the link beads twice more to strengthen the connection to the loop.

Finish the thread ends neatly and securely.

34 Make the Flowers and the Bees - Following steps 11 to 16 make three small daisies.

Referring to the bee instructions on pages 59 and 60 in the Sunflower Necklace chapter, and using black thread, make two bees. Finish off the shorter thread end on each bee leaving the longer ends to attach them to the bracelet.

Attach the Motifs - Arrange the flowers and bees along the length of the bracelet - you may want to make another flower if you have made a longer bracelet.

Stitch the daisies on first, using the attached thread end and adding 1C into the centre of each to finish neatly.

Finally add the bees and finish off all remaining thread ends neatly and securely.

Honeycomb Inspiration
Bee Hive Box

You Will Need

To Make the Bee Hive Box

7g of DB1458 silver lined light honey opal Delica beads A
10g of DB2177 semi-frost silver lined mica Delica beads B
0.4g of size 15/0 lustre yellow seed beads F
0.4g of size 15/0 frost transparent brown seed beads G
0.8g of size 15/0 silver lined crystal seed beads H
Two 4mm black fire polished faceted beads K
Two size 6/0 black seed beads L
0.4g of size 11/0 frost black seed beads M
6g of ceylon cream Twin beads P
4g of silver lined pale honey Twin beads Q
Grey and black size D beading thread

hive measures 40mm wide & 45mm high

35 Referring to steps 1 to 10 make the following hexagons -

One hexagon with 13A sides and P beads at the corners
One hexagon with 13B sides and Q beads at the corners
One hexagon with 11A sides and P beads at the corners
One hexagon with 11B sides and Q beads at the corners
One hexagon with 9B sides and Q beads at the corners
One hexagon with 7A sides and P beads at the corners
One hexagon with 5B sides and Q beads at the corners

36 Two hexagons with even bead count sides are also required -

One hexagon with 12B sides and Q beads at the corners.
One hexagon with 10A sides and P beads at the corners.

Although an even bead count means that it is easier to turn the needle at the end of each row of peyote stitch (as figs 6 and 7) it makes the corners of the hexagons a little more awkward. The thread at the start of the third tube will not line up with the link between the first and second tubes (as in step 8) - it's a half-a-bead width out.

Alternate the links to be half-a-bead out of line to one side and then the other (see fig 52 which shows the links longer than necessary for clarity). Adding the Twin beads to the outer corners through the beads opposite the links (as in step 10) will bring the tubes into a neat hexagon.

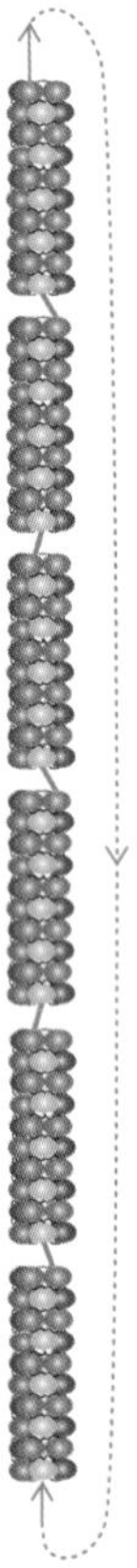

37 Make two stacks of hexagons lining up the Twin beads at the corners -

Stack One (from the bottom upwards) - The hexagons with sides of 13B, 13A, 12B, 11A, 11B and 10A. This will be the main unit of the box.

Stack Two (from the bottom upwards) - The hexagons with sides of 9B, 7A and 5B. This will be the lid of the box.

fig 52

Starting with Stack One, use the attached thread ends to stitch the Twin beads together at the corners. Make the stitches between the inner holes of the Twin beads so the hexagons are held closely together (fig 53). Work opposite corners in turn to ensure the stack does not distort.

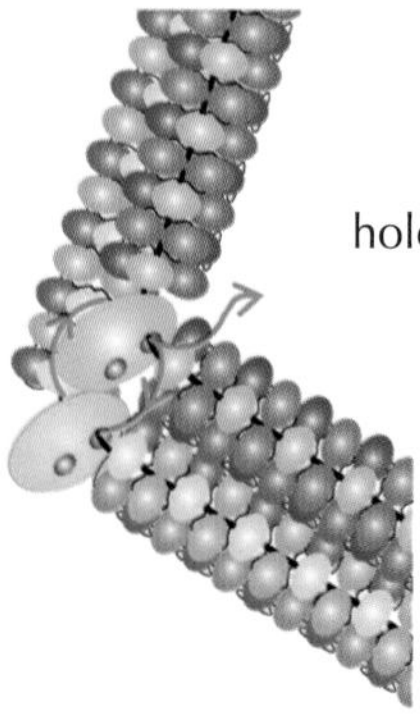

fig 53

For Stack Two stitch the outer holes of the Q beads on the 5B hexagon to the inner hole of the P beads on the 7A hexagon (fig 54).
Repeat to attach the outer holes of the P beads on the 7A hexagon to the inner holes on the Q beads of the 9B hexagon.

Finish off the thread ends neatly and securely.

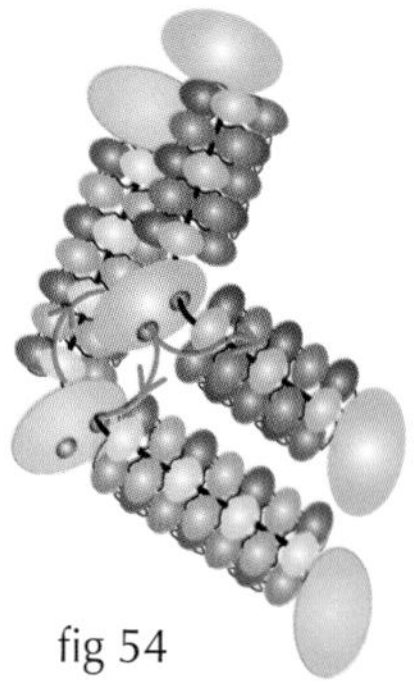

fig 54

fig 55

fig 56

38 Finishing the Lid - Prepare the needle with 80cm of single thread and thread on 6P. Pass the needle through the first hole to make a ring. Reinforce with a second pass of thread (fig 55).

Pass to the outer holes of the Twin beads and add 2A in each gap (fig 56).

fig 57

39 Pass through the first 1A of the first 2A stitch and thread on 1A. Pass the needle down the centre of the P bead ring and back through the new A bead to catch the thread in the gap between the P beads (fig 57).

Pass through the second A bead of the 2A stitch and the following P (fig 58). Repeat five times.

fig 58

Passing through the inner holes of the P bead ring stitch 1A across the central hole of the ring.

Stitch the finished disc into the centre of the 5B hexagon aligning the P beads of the disc with the corners of the lid. Finish off the thread ends neatly and securely.

the base of the hive

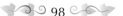

40 Making the Base - This is made using a similar method to the daisies (steps 11 to 16) but starting with a ring of P beads in the centre.

Mix a pinch of A and B together to make a mix (R) for the box base. Repeat step 38 using P and R beads.

Pass the needle through the first 1R of the first 2R stitch and thread on 2R. Pass through the next R around to pull the new 2R into the gap making a V-shape (fig 59). Pass through the next 1P and 1R.

fig 59

Repeat five more times to add 2R to each 2R of the previous row. Pass the needle through to emerge from the first R of the row just completed (fig 60).

fig 60

41 Thread on 2R. Pass down the next R and thread on 2R. Pass through the top R of the next column (fig 61).

Repeat to the end of the row and pass the needle through to emerge from the first R of the row just completed (fig 62).

fig 61

42 Thread on 2R. Pass down the next 2R and up the first R of the next 2R stitch.

Thread on 2R. Pass through the next R to start a new column and up the top 2R of the next column around (fig 63).

Repeat to the end of the row. You will have twelve columns - six are 4R high and six are 2R high (fig 64).

fig 62

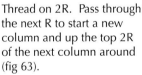
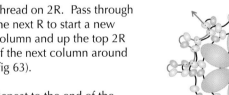

fig 63

43 Referring to the techniques in steps 17 and 18 extend the 4R columns to 7R high with an additional 3R petal tip.

Extend the 2R columns to 5R high with an additional 3R petal tip (fig 65).

fig 64

Aligning the longer columns with the corners of the 13B hexagon stitch the tips of the twelve columns to this hexagon to form the base of the box.

fig 65

44 The Legs - Start a 4B long peyote tube following steps 1 to 5. Add four more rows and zip into a tube. This wider tube has a hollow core - fill it with four loose B beads to make the tube more rigid and secure these extra filler beads with a couple of stitches.
Place the tube at one corner of the box base to cover the corner of the hexagon and the attachment of the column from step 43. Stitch into place firmly and finish off the thread ends neatly and securely.
Repeat to complete and attach five more legs.

45 Completing the Hive Box - Making the Hinges - Attach a new thread to emerge from the outer hole of a Q bead on the 9B hexagon of the lid.
Line up this Q bead with a P bead from the top hexagon of the base unit and stitch together the outer two holes.
Make two stitches between the outer hole of the P bead and the inner hole of the Q bead to stabilise the hinge.

Repeat to make a hinge from the next P and Q beads around the box and lid. Finish off the thread ends neatly and securely.

Referring to the bee instructions on pages 59 and 60 in the Sunflower Necklace chapter, and using black thread, make two bees. Finish off the shorter thread end on each bee leaving the longer ends to attach them to the box. Stitch the bees onto the box in the position of your choice.

Sinensis
Necklace

✿✿✿✿

necklace length 47cm

Waterfalls

of tanzanite and pearl-white racemes of tiny slipper-shaped blooms break out with the warming sun of spring to smother hitherto bare vines.

Use spring green, ochre and lemon seed beads for the racemes to change them into willowy catkins.

The Necklace is Made in Six Stages

The central floral raceme is made first.
The technique is repeated to make all the racemes and links on either side of the centre front.
The links between the raceme groups are converted into arches.
The side straps are made and attached.
The leaf motifs are made and attached.
The crystal strand is added to complete the design.

1 The First Raceme - Prepare the needle with 1.5m of single thread and tie a keeper bead 15cm from the end.

Thread on 18L, 1B, 3G, 19H and 7A. Leaving aside the last 3A beads to anchor the strand pass the needle back up through the preceding 3A (fig 1).

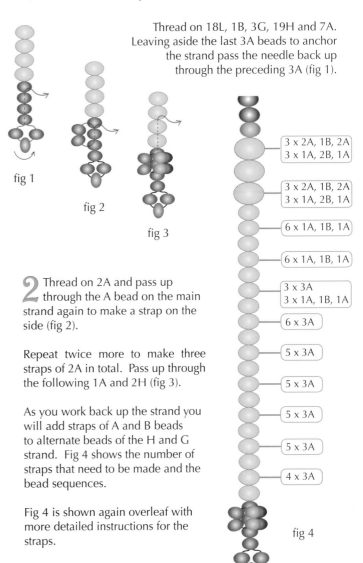

fig 1

fig 2

fig 3

3 x 2A, 1B, 2A
3 x 1A, 2B, 1A

3 x 2A, 1B, 2A
3 x 1A, 2B, 1A

6 x 1A, 1B, 1A

6 x 1A, 1B, 1A

3 x 3A
3 x 1A, 1B, 1A

6 x 3A

5 x 3A

5 x 3A

5 x 3A

5 x 3A

4 x 3A

fig 4

2 Thread on 2A and pass up through the A bead on the main strand again to make a strap on the side (fig 2).

Repeat twice more to make three straps of 2A in total. Pass up through the following 1A and 2H (fig 3).

As you work back up the strand you will add straps of A and B beads to alternate beads of the H and G strand. Fig 4 shows the number of straps that need to be made and the bead sequences.

Fig 4 is shown again overleaf with more detailed instructions for the straps.

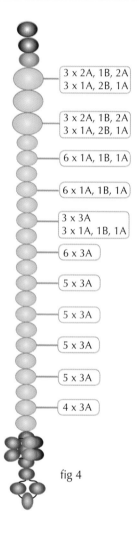

3 × 2A, 1B, 2A
3 × 1A, 2B, 1A

3 × 2A, 1B, 2A
3 × 1A, 2B, 1A

6 × 1A, 1B, 1A

6 × 1A, 1B, 1A

3 × 3A
3 × 1A, 1B, 1A

6 × 3A

5 × 3A

5 × 3A

5 × 3A

5 × 3A

4 × 3A

fig 4

3 Refer to fig 4 throughout and ensure that each strap pulls in neatly to the main strand bead that supports it.

Add four straps of 3A to the current H bead. Pass up through the following 2H.

Add five straps of 3A to the current H bead. Pass up through the following 2H. Repeat three times to emerge from the twelfth H bead from the bottom of the strand.

Add six straps of 3A to the current H bead. Pass up through the following 2H.

Add three straps of 3A and three straps of 1A, 1B and 1A to alternate around the current H bead. Pass up through the following 2H.

Add six straps of 1A, 1B and 1A to the current H bead Pass up through the following 2H. Repeat once and pass up through the following 1H and 1G beads.

Add three straps of 2A, 1B and 2A and three straps of 1A, 2B and 1A to alternate around the G bead. Pass up through the following 2G and repeat the same alternating straps once more (fig 5).

Pass up through the following 1B and 18L to emerge at the keeper bead.

All the racemes follow this method albeit with different length strands and colour combinations.

fig 5

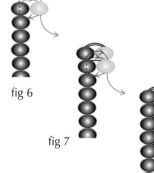

fig 6

fig 7

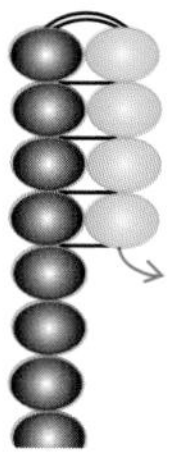

fig 8

4 Thread on 1N. Pass back up through the previous L bead and back down the new N bead to bring the two beads together with the holes parallel (fig 6).

Thread on 1N. Pass the needle up the next L bead and down through the new N (fig 7). This is square stitch.

Repeat to square stitch 1N to each of the next 2L (fig 8).

5 Repeating the Technique - Thread on 7N, 1D, 3K, 19L and 7C. This is the stem for the second raceme.

Leaving aside the last 3C beads to anchor the strand pass the needle back up through the preceding 3C (as fig 1). Add 3 x 2C straps to this bead (as fig 3) and pass up through the following 1C and 2L.

Fig 9 shows the strap sequences for this raceme. Add the straps in C and D beads as shown.

When the eleven sets of straps are complete, pass the needle up through the remaining 1D and 11N (fig 10).

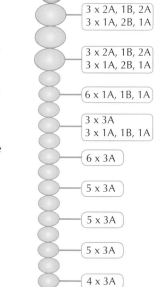

3 x 2C, 1D, 2C
3 x 1C, 2D, 1C

3 x 2C, 1D, 2C
3 x 1C, 2D, 1C

6 x 1C, 1D, 1C

6 x 1C, 1D, 1C

3 x 3C
3 x 1C, 1D, 1C

6 x 3C

5 x 3C

5 x 3C

5 x 3C

5 x 3C

4 x 3C

fig 9

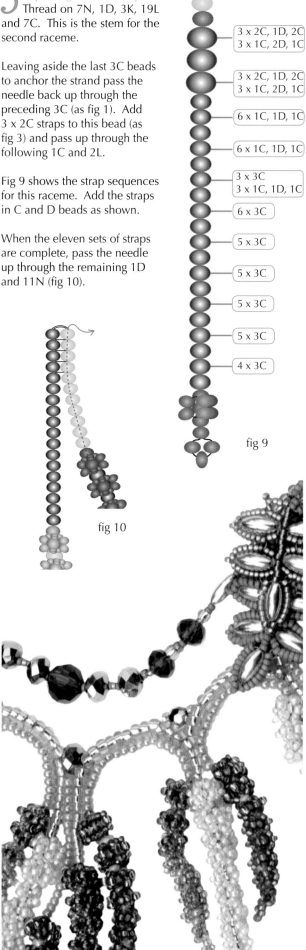

fig 10

6 Following the technique in step 4, square stitch 1L to each of the top 4N beads of the stem just completed (fig 11).

Thread on 1B, 3G, 15H and 7A. This is the stem for the third raceme.

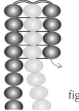

fig 11

As before, leave aside the last 3A to anchor the strand and pass back up the preceding 3A (as fig 1). Add 3 x 2A straps (as fig 3) and pass up through the following 1A and 2H.

7 Fig 12 shows the strap sequence for this raceme. Add ten sets of straps in A and B beads as shown.

Finish with the needle emerging from the first L bead of this stem (fig 13).

Thread on 13L for the link to the next raceme group.

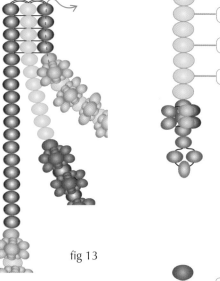

3 x 2A, 1B, 2A
3 x 1A, 2B, 1A

3 x 2A, 1B, 2A
3 x 1A, 2B, 1A

6 x 1A, 1B, 1A

3 x 3A
3 x 1A, 1B, 1A

6 x 3A

5 x 3A

5 x 3A

5 x 3A

4 x 3A

fig 12

fig 13

8 Thread on 4L, 1D, 1K, 13L and 7C for the stem of the fourth raceme.

Make the anchor at the bottom as fig 1 and add 3 x 2C straps as fig 3.

Fig 14 shows the strap sequences for this raceme. Add the straps in C and D beads as shown.

Pass the needle through the 1D and 4L beads above the K bead after making the top set of straps.

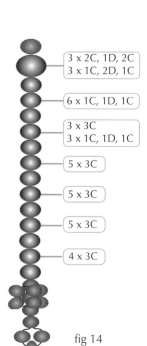

3 x 2C, 1D, 2C
3 x 1C, 2D, 1C

6 x 1C, 1D, 1C

3 x 3C
3 x 1C, 1D, 1C

5 x 3C

5 x 3C

5 x 3C

4 x 3C

fig 14

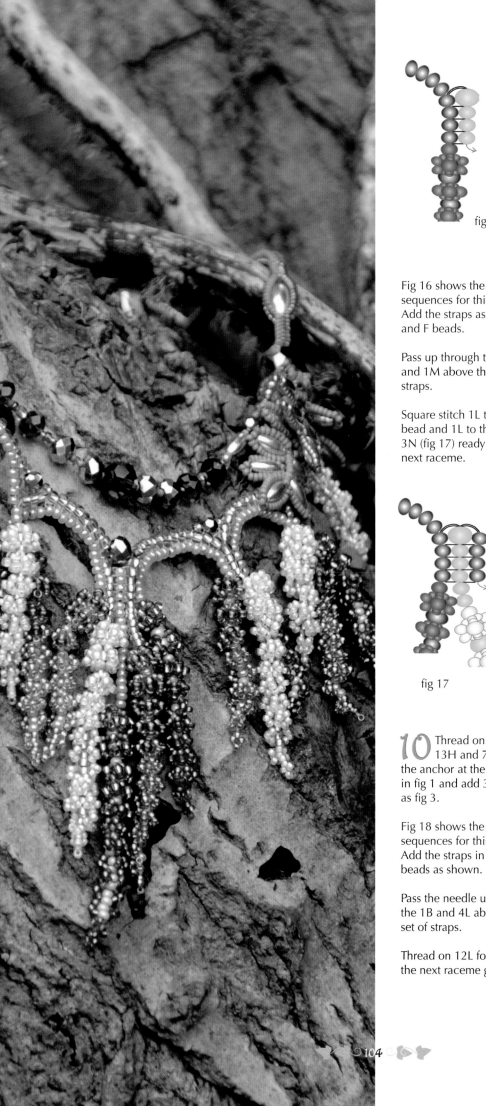

9 Square stitch 1M to this L bead and 1N to the next 3L (fig 15) ready to start the next raceme.

Thread on 2N, 1F, 3M, 15N and 7E. Make the anchor at the bottom as fig 1 and add 3 x 2E straps as fig 3.

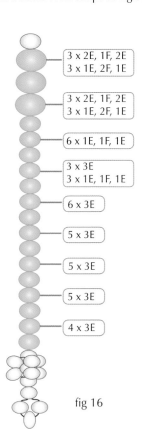

fig 15

Fig 16 shows the strap sequences for this raceme. Add the straps as shown in E and F beads.

Pass up through the 1F, 5N and 1M above the last set of straps.

Square stitch 1L to the M bead and 1L to the following 3N (fig 17) ready to start the next raceme.

	3 x 2E, 1F, 2E
	3 x 1E, 2F, 1E
	3 x 2E, 1F, 2E
	3 x 1E, 2F, 1E
	6 x 1E, 1F, 1E
	3 x 3E
	3 x 1E, 1F, 1E
	6 x 3E
	5 x 3E
	5 x 3E
	5 x 3E
	4 x 3E

fig 16

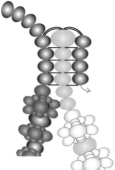

fig 17

10 Thread on 1B, 1G, 13H and 7A. Make the anchor at the bottom as in fig 1 and add 3 x 2A straps as fig 3.

Fig 18 shows the strap sequences for this raceme. Add the straps in A and B beads as shown.

Pass the needle up through the 1B and 4L above the last set of straps.

Thread on 12L for the link to the next raceme group.

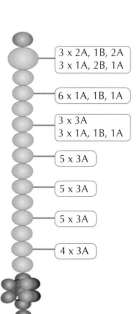

	3 x 2A, 1B, 2A
	3 x 1A, 2B, 1A
	6 x 1A, 1B, 1A
	3 x 3A
	3 x 1A, 1B, 1A
	5 x 3A
	5 x 3A
	5 x 3A
	4 x 3A

fig 18

11 Thread on 4L, 1F, 1M, 11N and 7E for the first raceme of this group.

Make the anchor as in fig 1 and add 3 x 2E straps as in fig 3.

Fig 19 shows the strap sequences for this raceme. Add the straps in E and F beads as shown.

Pass the needle up through the 1F and 4L above the last set of straps. Repeat fig 15 to square stitch 1M and 3N to the top 4L beads.

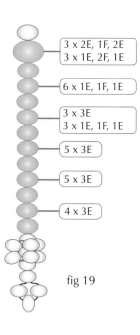

3 x 2E, 1F, 2E
3 x 1E, 2F, 1E

6 x 1E, 1F, 1E

3 x 3E
3 x 1E, 1F, 1E

5 x 3E

5 x 3E

4 x 3E

fig 19

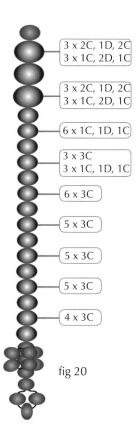

3 x 2C, 1D, 2C
3 x 1C, 2D, 1C

3 x 2C, 1D, 2C
3 x 1C, 2D, 1C

6 x 1C, 1D, 1C

3 x 3C
3 x 1C, 1D, 1C

6 x 3C

5 x 3C

5 x 3C

5 x 3C

4 x 3C

fig 20

12 Thread on 1N, 1D, 3K, 15L and 7C. Make the anchor as in fig 1 and add 3 x 2C straps as fig 3.

Fig 20 shows the strap sequences for this raceme. Add the straps in C and D beads as shown.

Pass up through the 1D, 4N and 1M above the last set of straps.

Square stitch 4L to the top 1M and 3N ready to start the next raceme.

13 Thread on 2L, 1B, 1G, 13H and 7A. Make the anchor as in fig 1 and add 3 x 2A straps as in fig 3.

Fig 21 shows the strap sequences for this raceme. Add the straps as shown in A and B beads.

Pass the needle up through the 1B and 6L above the top strap sequence.

Thread on 12L for the link to the next raceme.

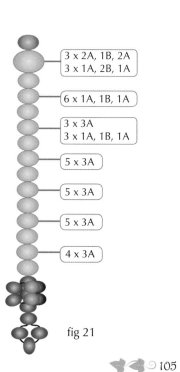

3 x 2A, 1B, 2A
3 x 1A, 2B, 1A

6 x 1A, 1B, 1A

3 x 3A
3 x 1A, 1B, 1A

5 x 3A

5 x 3A

5 x 3A

4 x 3A

fig 21

14 Repeat step 11.

There is no raceme attached to the bottom of the 3N just added. Square stitch 1L to each of the 3N and 1M just added. Thread on 14L (18L added in total).

Pass the needle through the third and second L beads of the 18L just added, to point towards the start of the sequence and form a loop (fig 22).

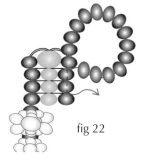

fig 22

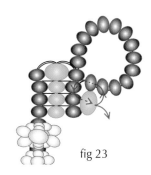

fig 23

Thread on 1M and square stitch to the 18th L bead so the new bead sits on the outside of the loop (fig 23).

Square stitch 1M to each of the following 4L.

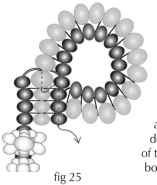

fig 24

15 Thread on 2M and square stitch to the next L bead (fig 24).

Make three more single M bead stitches to the next 3L and a 2M stitch to the following 1L.

Make four more single stitches and pass the needle down the M bead at the top of the raceme group.

Weave the needle across one row and pass down through the first 3L of the 18L to emerge at the bottom of the row (fig 25).

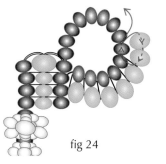

fig 25

16 Thread on 1L, 1B, 1G, 7H and 7A.

Referring to fig 26 make the anchor at the bottom and add the straps to complete the last raceme on this side of the centrepiece.

Pass the needle up through the following 1B and 2L. Weave across to the adjacent row and up through the 1N and 1M to emerge at the top of the centre row of the raceme group.

Remove the needle and leave the thread end loose.

Return to the first row worked in step 1 and prepare the needle with a new 1.5m single thread length.

3 x 3A
3 x 1A, 1B, 1A

5 x 3A

5 x 3A

4 x 3A

fig 26

17 Pass the needle up through the top 10L of the 18L added in step 1 to emerge at the top of the row alongside the first keeper bead.

Square stitch 4N to the top 4L just passed through (fig 27).

Thread on 4N, 1F, 3M, 19N and 7E to start the first raceme on this side of the centrepiece. Make the anchor as fig 1 and add 3 x 2E straps as fig 3.

Using E and F beads, instead of A and B beads, complete this raceme using the same strap counts as fig 4.

Pass up through the 1F and 8N above the last set of straps.

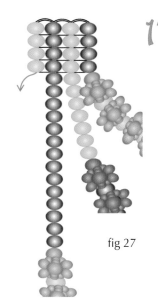

fig 27

18 Add 4L square stitches to the top 4N to begin the fifth raceme of the central group.

Thread on 1D, 1K, 13L and 7C. Make the raceme as in fig 14 passing through the 1D and 4N above the last set of straps.

Thread on 13L to make the link to the next raceme group.

19 The following three raceme groups are a reflection of the other side of the design albeit with a change in the colour sequence.

Repeat from steps 8 to 16 to make a mirror image of the raceme sequences, links and end loop with the following colour substitutions.

Make the first group with -
Raceme one in A, B, G and H
Raceme two in C, D, K and L
Raceme three in E, F, M and N

Make the second group with -
Raceme one in C, D, K and L
Raceme two in A, B, G and H
Raceme three in E, F, M and N

Make the third group with -
Raceme one in C, D, K and L
Raceme two - blank
Raceme three in E, F, M and N

Reposition the needle as in step 16 to emerge from the M bead at the top of the raceme group. You now work across the links, between the raceme groups, to create the arches.

20 Making the Arches - Thread on 1M. Square stitch this 1M to the adjacent 1M at the base of the loop (fig 28).

Square stitch this new M to the first L bead of the link (fig 29).

Square stitch 1M to each of the following 11L along the link (fig 30).

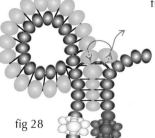

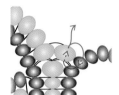

fig 28

fig 29

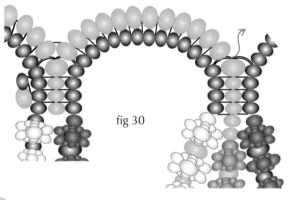

fig 30

23 Strengthening the Top Line - The arched links need to be reinforced with further passes of thread.

Referring to fig 33 weave across to the adjacent outside L bead row and pass through the L beads of that arch into the next raceme group. Weave across to the N beads of the square stitched block and up through the N and M at the top.

Pass through the M beads of the arch just worked (fig 33).

Pass the needle back through the L bead arch and up through the M beads of the next arch along. Pass back through the L beads.

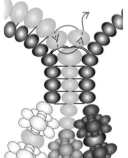

21 Square stitch 1M to the last M (fig 31).

Square stitch this M to the corresponding 1L at the start of the next 12L link (as fig 29).

fig 31

22 Square stitch 1M to each of the following 11L and repeat step 21.

Square stitch 1M to the following 12L. Pass the needle down the top N bead of the first raceme group (fig 32).

Remove the needle and let the thread hang loose.

Repeat steps 20 to 22 with the thread end from step 16 at the other end of the work.

Leave the needle attached.

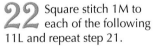

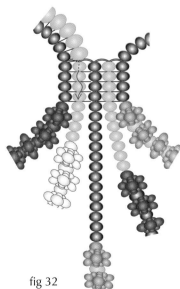

fig 32

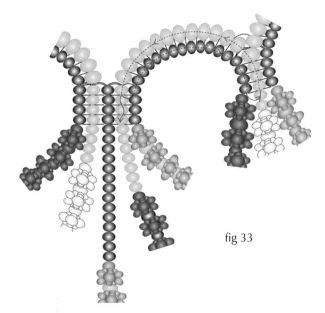

fig 33

Pass back through the M beads of this arch once more.

Repeat to strengthen the last arch on this side of the design and the end loop. Remove the needle leaving the thread loose.

Repeat with the other thread end from step 22 to strengthen the other side of the centrepiece.

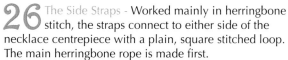

26 The Side Straps - Worked mainly in herringbone stitch, the straps connect to either side of the necklace centrepiece with a plain, square stitched loop. The main herringbone rope is made first.

Prepare the needle with 1.8m of single thread with a keeper bead 50cm from the end. Thread on 1P, 1Q, 1P and 1Q. Pass the needle through the first P to make a ring (fig 37).

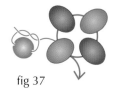

fig 37

Pass the needle through the four beads again to strengthen the ring. Using this ring as the base for a four-bead herringbone stitch rope, work ten rows of 1P, 1Q and 1P, 1Q.

24 If necessary attach a new 75cm single thread to emerge from the 13th M bead of an end loop pointing back along the top row of arches (fig 34).

Thread on 1N, 1R and 1N. Pass through the fourth M bead and the following 5M of the adjacent arch (fig 35).

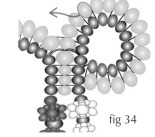

fig 34

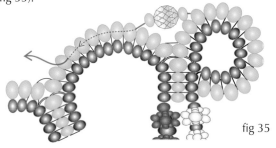

fig 35

27 The rope now divides to accommodate a Z bead (which will be added in step 32).

The needle should be emerging from a P bead. Thread on 13P.

Square stitch 1Q to each P to make a parallel row of 13Q. Pass the needle up the first 13P and down the 13Q to bring them into line (see fig 38).

Pass the needle down the following Q bead on the end of the rope and up through the next P around the end of the rope (fig 38).

Repeat step 27 to make a second strap of 13P and 13Q.

Thread on 1N, 1R and 1N. Pass through the fourth M bead and the following 5M of the adjacent arch (as fig 35). Repeat once more.

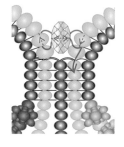

25 Pass through the next 3M and thread on 1S to bridge the central gap.

Pass up through the 2nd M bead on the opposite link, back through the S bead and the 2nd link M bead on this side of the S bead (fig 36).

fig 36

Pass through the S bead, the 2nd M on the link and through the following 8M ready to add the next 1N, 1R and 1N bridge between the arched links. Make the bridge and repeat in the final two gaps.

Pass the needle backwards and forwards through the row just added and the beads of the arches to make firm.

Finish off all remaining thread ends without blocking the bead holes around the loops at either end of the work.

28 Pass the needle up the first row of 13P and bring the two ends of the straps together to make a square of 1P, 1Q, 1P and 1Q.

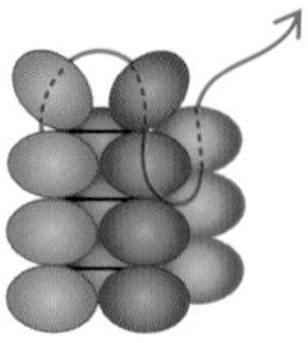

fig 38

Restart the herringbone stitch rope linking the two straps together (fig 39).

Work 26 rows of 1P, 1Q and 1P, 1Q.

fig 39

29 Thread on 1T. Restart the herringbone stitch after the T bead (passing the needle back and forth through the T bead twice, after the first two rows, to make sure the ends of the ropes are firmly pulled up to the T bead).

Work until the rope is the desired length.

back view

30 The Bead Tag - Thread on 1R, 1Q, 1B, 1V, 1B, 1M, 1D, 1W, 1D, 1M and 3Q. Leaving aside the last 3Q to anchor the strand pass the needle back through the previous M and the following beads to emerge at the end of the rope (fig 40).

fig 40

Pass the needle through the beads at the end of the rope and back and forth through the tag beads twice to strengthen. Finish off the thread neatly and securely.

31 Return to the keeper bead from step 26. Remove the keeper and attach the needle to the thread.

Thread on 1U and 25P. Square stitch 1Q to each P bead to make a strip 25 beads long and two beads wide. Pass back through the U bead (fig 41).

fig 41

Pass through the beads at the end of the rope and back through the U bead.
Pass the strip through the loop at one end of the centrepiece folding the strip back to the U bead to trap the loop and link the strap to the centrepiece.

Stitch the last P and Q of the square-stitch strip to the first P and Q to secure the link. Make sure the strap is firmly pulled up against the U bead and pass the needle through the 25 beads of each row of the strip to make it neat and strong.

Pass the needle back through the U bead to the rope side.

32 Place 1Z between the two sides of the split rope (made in step 27). Pass the needle up through the rope beads and secure the Z bead in place. Finish off the thread neatly and securely.

33 Repeat steps 26 to 29 to make a second herringbone rope - this rope needs the bead loop side of the clasp.

The Bead Loop - Thread on 1R, 1B and sufficient D beads to make a loop that will just fit over the V and W beads of the tag (approximately 19D).

Pass back through the B and R beads to pull up the loop (fig 42).

fig 42

Reinforce the loop with several passes of the needle and finish off the thread neatly and securely.

Repeat steps 31 and 32 to attach this side strap to the necklace centrepiece. Finish off all remaining thread ends neatly and securely.

34 The Leaves - Prepare the needle with 1.2m of single thread and tie a keeper bead 15cm from the end. Thread on 20P, 1Y and 3P.

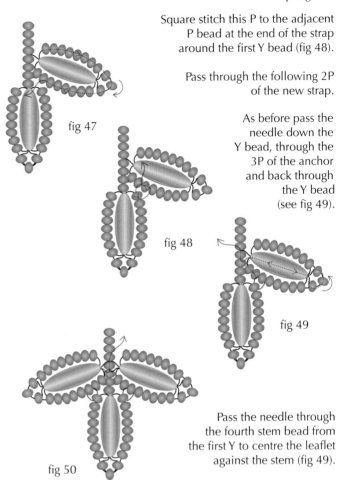

Leaving aside the last 3P to anchor the strand pass the needle back through the Y bead (fig 43).

fig 43

Thread on 8P and pass through the Y bead again to make a strap on one side. Repeat (fig 44).

fig 44

Pass the needle through the first 8P, the 3P of the anchor and the following strap of 8P to bring the frame around the Y bead into line (fig 45).

fig 45

fig 46

Pass the needle down the Y bead, through the 3P of the anchor and back up through the Y bead. Pass through the following 4P of the main stem (fig 46).

35 Thread on 1Y and 3P. Make the 3P anchor as before and the two straps of 8P. Pass through the first strap of 8P, the 3P of the anchor and the following 6P of the second strap (fig 47).

Square stitch this P to the adjacent P bead at the end of the strap around the first Y bead (fig 48).

fig 47

Pass through the following 2P of the new strap.

As before pass the needle down the Y bead, through the 3P of the anchor and back through the Y bead (see fig 49).

fig 48

fig 49

Pass the needle through the fourth stem bead from the first Y to centre the leaflet against the stem (fig 49).

fig 50

Repeat step 35 to make a second leaflet on the other side of the main stem (fig 50).

36 Pass up through the next 6P of the main stem and thread on 1Y and 3P to start the next leaflet. Make the leaflet as before linking the sixth P bead on this leaflet to the sixth P bead on the adjacent leaflet with a square stitch (fig 51).

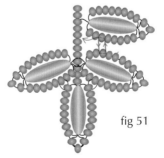

Pass through the same main stem bead to centre the leaflet. Repeat to make a matching leaflet on the other side of the main stem (fig 52).

fig 51

Repeat to add a third pair of leaflets.

Pass up through 4P of the main stem to emerge at the keeper bead.

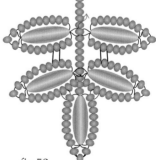

fig 52

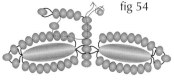

fig 53

fig 54

37 Thread on 5P. Leaving aside 1P to make an anchor pass back through the 4th P just added (fig 53).

Thread on 1P. Pass the needle through the first 3P of the frame on the adjacent leaflet and up the top 3P of the main stem (fig 54).

Repeat on the other side of the main stem. Remove the needle and set aside.

Repeat steps 34 to 37 to make a matching leaf using the Q beads. Leave the thread ends loose and remove the needle.

38 Prepare the needle as in step 34 and thread on 14P, 1Y and 3P. Complete a leaf motif on this shorter stem making two leaflets on either side and the smaller points on either side of the keeper bead (fig 55).

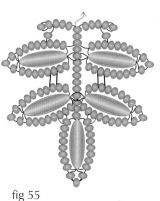

fig 55

Repeat step 38 to make one more small leaf in P and two small leaves in Q.

Leave the thread ends loose and remove the needle.

39 Divide the leaf motifs into two sets, one large and two small for each side of the design.

Work on one side at a time. Lay the large leaf along the top of the end arch, the first small leaf across the top of the large leaf from the top of the M bead loop and the third leaf from just below the U bead on the strap (fig 56).

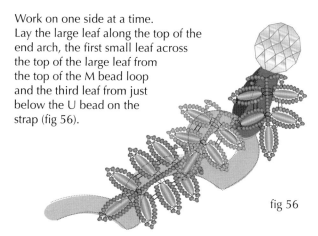

fig 56

Adjust the positions until the effect pleases and stitch the leaves into place with the thread tails. Use sufficient small stitches to hold the stems fast but allow the leaflets to hang as free as possible. Do not finish thread ends yet.

40 The Crystal Strand - Prepare the needle with 75cm of doubled thread and tie a keeper bead 15cm from the end.

Thread on 3P, 1M, 2Q, 1R, 1Q, 1Y, 2Q, 1M, 1P, 1T, 1Q, 1D, 1M, 1T, 1P, 1D, 1P, 1S, 1Q, 1P, 1Q, 1S, 1Q and 1X. This X is the centre of the sequence. Reverse the threading order to make the string symmetrical on either side of the X bead.

Pass the needle up through the fifth M bead of one of the end loops made in steps 14 and 15 (fig 57).

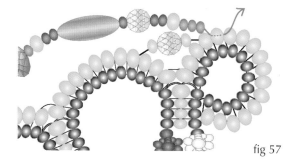

fig 57

Hold the keeper bead against the corresponding M bead on the other side of the design. Now flex the necklace centre slightly to fall into a shallow curve and then into a deeper U-shape - you will see the crystal row move towards and away from the beaded arches depending on the width/depth of the curve of the centrepiece.

Place the whole necklace down in the shape it will sit around your neck and look at the position of the crystal string - is it sitting 12-14mm above the arches, or much higher leaving an awkward gap. If it is, you need to add a few P beads to either end of the crystal strand. If the opposite is true and it clashes against the arches: remove a few P beads and try again.

When the strand is sitting correctly pass the needle through a further 3-4 beads and finish off the thread neatly and securely. Remove the keeper bead and repeat, threading up through the correct beads on the other side of the design.

Finish off all remaining thread ends neatly and securely.

Index & Suppliers

All of the materials used in this book should be available in any good bead shop or online. If you are new to beading, or need more supplies, the companies listed below run fast, efficient mail order services, hold large stocks of all of the materials you will need in their stores and give good, well-informed friendly advice on aspects of beading and beading needs.

In the UK

Spellbound Bead Co
47 Tamworth Street,
Lichfield
Staffordshire
WS13 6JW
01543 417650

www.spellboundbead.co.uk

Spellbound Bead Co supplied all of the materials for the samples shown. You can buy the beads loose (wholesale and retail) or in kits (with or without instructions), for all of the designs you see here.

In USA

Fire Mountain Gems
One Fire Mountain Way
Grants Pass
OR 97526 - 2373
Tel: + 800 355 2137
www.firemountaingems.com

Shipwreck Beads
8560 Commerce Place Dr.NE
Lacey
WA 98516
Tel: + 800 950 4232
www.shipwreckbeads.com